TABLE OF CONTENTS:

https://www.canva.com/design/DAFyMiOOK9Y/4bvQ2NGXLtcriZKPvgyAgQ/watch?utm_content=DAFyMiOOK9Y&utm_campaign=share_your_design&utm_medium=link&utm_source=shareyourdesignpanel

All these recipes are perfect to be enjoyed immediately or prepared in advance for your weekly meal prep, ensuring freshness and flavor every time you savor them.

information contained within this book. Either directly or indirectly.

Legal Notice:

Disclaimer Notice:

INTRODUCTION

Welcome to "Healthy Meal Prep: The Recipe Book for a Healthy and Delicious Life." This book has been created with the goal of providing you with a culinary experience that satisfies not only your taste buds but also your overall well-being. Healthy cooking should never be boring or tasteless, and here you will find a variety of delicious dishes that will help you maintain a balanced lifestyle.

Healthy meal preparation is much more than a trend; it's a philosophy that promotes self-care through nutrition. In this recipe book, you will discover a world of culinary options that allow you to plan your meals in advance, save time, and improve your health. Whether you are an experienced cooking enthusiast or a beginner in search of inspiration, there's something for everyone.

Every recipe presented in this book has been carefully selected for its deliciousness and health benefits. We have included options for nutritious breakfasts, tasty appetizers, main dishes with meat and fish, wholesome side dishes, delightful snacks, and healthy treats. Each recipe is designed to be both flavorful and nourishing, contributing to your overall well-being.

Maintaining a healthy lifestyle doesn't mean sacrificing taste or variety. With our recipes, you will discover that you can enjoy delicious foods without guilt. Furthermore, meal preparation will help you better manage your diet, avoid impulsive food choices, and stay in control of what you put into your body.

Good Healthy Habits at the Table and Beyond

In addition to the delicious recipes presented in this book, we want to share some good habits that will contribute to your overall well-being. Maintaining a healthy lifestyle goes beyond what you put on your plate. Here are some habits to keep in mind:

Mindful Eating: Take the time to savor every bite. Eating slowly helps you recognize your body's satiety signals and avoid overeating.

Stay Hydrated: Water is essential for your body. Make sure to stay hydrated by drinking enough throughout the day.

Choose Whole Foods: Opt for whole foods like whole grains, legumes, and vegetables. They are rich in nutrients and fiber, keeping you full and satisfied.

Limit Added Sugars: Minimize the consumption of sugary foods and drinks. Replace them with naturally sweet options like fruit.

Meal Preparation: Meal prep helps you avoid impulsive food choices. Plan your meals in advance and prepare healthy foods to take with you.

Exercise: Combining good nutrition with physical activity is crucial for maintaining health. Try to be active every day.

Maintain Balance: Indulge in occasional culinary pleasures, but aim for overall balance in your diet.

These healthy habits will help support your goal of a healthy and delicious life. Now, get ready to embark on your culinary journey to well-being!

Ready to start your journey towards a healthier and more delicious life? Prepare your kitchen, purchase the ingredients, and get ready to experience the wonderful recipes of "Healthy Meal Prep." Your health and taste buds will thank you. Let the culinary adventure begin!

Guidelines for creating effective meal prep:

Planning: Planning is crucial. Start by planning the meals you want to prepare, deciding on recipes, and creating a grocery list.

Choose Balanced Meals: Make sure your meals include lean protein, complex carbohydrates, vegetables, and healthy fats. This combination will help keep you full and nourished.

Choose Simple Recipes: To simplify the meal prep process, opt for recipes that are easy to prepare and store.

Organization: Organize your workspace in the kitchen. Ensure you have all the ingredients, freezer or storage containers, and equipment like pots, pans, and blenders ready.

Ingredient Preparation: Before you start cooking, wash, chop, and prepare all the ingredients. This will make the cooking process smoother.

Batch Cooking: Prepare large quantities of food at once. For example, you can grill a big batch of chicken or cook a lot of quinoa.

Portioning: Once cooked, divide the meals into individual portions. Use airtight containers to keep them fresh.

Labeling: Label the containers with the meal name and preparation date. This will help you keep track of freshness.

Freezing: If you're preparing meals for an extended period, you can freeze them. Make sure to use freezer-safe containers.

Variation: Prepare different meals to avoid boredom. Change up the recipes, proteins, and vegetables to maintain interest.

Serving: Decide if the meals will be ready to eat directly from the fridge or if they will require a brief cooking or reheating.

Storage: Store prepared meals in the fridge or freezer, depending on the expected duration.

Monitoring: Keep track of the preparation date and preferred consumption date for each meal to avoid waste.

Convenience: Organize meals so they are easy to grab when you need a quick meal.

Hygiene: Ensure you follow proper food hygiene practices during meal preparation and storage.

Supplies: Make sure you always have key ingredients on hand to simplify the preparation process.

Meal prep is a fantastic strategy to save time, money, and eat healthier. By following these guidelines, you can prepare delicious and convenient meals that will be ready when you need them.

Plan Your Meals: Decide what you'll prepare, and create a meal plan Choose recipes that are easy to make in bulk.

Shopping List: Create a shopping list based on your meal plan. This helps you buy exactly what you need and minimizes waste.

Storage Containers: Invest in good-quality, airtight containers for storing your prepared meals. These should be microwave-safe and stackable.

Batch Cooking: Prepare larger quantities of food at once to save time. For example, cook a big pot of rice or grill a lot of chicken.

Protein Options: Cook a variety of proteins (chicken, beef, tofu, etc.) so you can mix and match throughout the week.

Vegetable Prep: Wash, chop, and prepare vegetables in advance. Store them in airtight containers or resealable bags.

Portion Control: Divide your meals into portion-sized containers to prevent overeating. This also makes it easy to grab a meal and go.

Labeling: Label containers with the contents and the date of preparation. This ensures you use them before they go bad.

Freezing: If you're meal prepping for an extended period, freeze the meals in appropriate containers. Some meals can be frozen for up to 3 months.

Fridge Storage: Meals stored in the fridge should generally be consumed within 3-4 days. Consider investing in glass containers for longer-lasting freshness.

Freezer Storage: Properly stored, frozen meals can last for 2-3 months. Use freezer-safe containers and ensure they are well-sealed to prevent freezer burn.

Microwave-Safe Containers: Look for containers labeled as "microwave-safe" for reheating. Glass containers with microwave-safe lids are a popular choice.

BPA-Free Containers: Consider BPA-free plastic or glass containers, especially for meals that will be heated in the microwave.

Consider Mason Jars: Mason jars work well for salads and layered dishes. Just remember to pack the dressing separately.

Prep Containers for Cooking: Use oven-safe glass containers when preparing meals that need reheating in the oven.

Keep Sauces Separate: When storing meals with sauces or dressings, consider using separate containers to keep the food from getting soggy.

Safety First: Follow proper food safety and hygiene practices during meal prep to ensure the safety and quality of your meals.

Quick Reheating: Opt for meals that can be reheated quickly in the microwave if you're short on time.

Variety: Keep your meal prep interesting by rotating recipes and trying new dishes.

Hydration: Don't forget to prep drinks like infused water or iced tea for a refreshing addition to your meals.

Remember that while these tips provide general guidelines, it's essential to use your judgment and adapt them to your specific needs and preferences. Properly storing and reheating your meals will help you make the most of your meal prep efforts.

- *Difficulty Level:* □□□
- *Preparation Time: 10 minutes*
- *Cooking Time: 15 minutes*
- *Cooking Skill: Medium*

Ingredients:

- *1 cup whole wheat flour*
- *2 tablespoons sugar*
- *1 teaspoon baking powder*
- *1/2 teaspoon baking soda*
- *1/4 teaspoon salt*
- *1 cup milk (you can choose regular milk, almond milk, or soy milk)*
- *1 egg*
- *2 tablespoons vegetable oil*
- *Fresh berries (strawberries, blueberries, blackberries, etc.)*
- *Honey or maple syrup for drizzling (optional)*

Instructions:

- *In a bowl, mix the whole wheat flour, sugar, baking powder, baking soda, and salt.*
- *In another bowl, beat the egg, then add the milk and vegetable oil. Mix well.*

Directions:

1. *Pour the liquid mixture into the bowl with the dry ingredients and mix until you have a smooth batter. Be careful not to overmix; it's okay if there are some lumps.*
2. *Heat a non-stick skillet over medium heat and lightly grease it with oil or butter.*
3. *Pour a ladle of batter into the skillet to form a pancake. Cook until bubbles appear on the surface, then flip and cook on the other side until golden*

BREAKFAST:

SWEET OPTIONS:

Whole Wheat Pancakes with Fresh Berries

brown. Cooking time will vary, but it's usually about 2-3 minutes per side.

4. Repeat the process with the remaining batter.
5. Serve the pancakes hot, topped with fresh berries and, if desired, a drizzle of honey or maple syrup.
6. Tips:
7. You can add a handful of fresh berries directly into the batter before cooking the pancakes to make them even more delicious.
8. If you want to keep the pancakes warm while preparing the rest, you can place them in an oven at a low temperature (around 200°F) on a plate covered with aluminum foil.

Nutritional Information (per pancake):

Calories: 105

Protein: 3g

Fat: 4g

Carbohydrates: 15g

Fiber: 2g

Sugar: 4g

Glycemic Index (GI): The glycemic index of whole wheat pancakes is moderate thanks to the use of whole wheat flour. Adding fresh berries and a moderate amount of sugar helps maintain the GI at an acceptable level. However, if you want to further reduce the GI, you can skip the sugar or use low-GI sweeteners.

Oatmeal with Blueberries and Walnuts (for Two)

- *Difficulty Level:* ☐
- *Preparation Time: 5 minutes*
- *Cooking Time: 10 minutes*
- *Cooking Skill: Easy*

Ingredients:

- *1 cup of oats*
- *2 cups of milk (you can choose between regular milk, almond milk, or soy milk)*
- *1/2 cup of fresh or frozen blueberries*
- *1/4 cup of chopped walnuts*
- *1 tablespoon of honey or maple syrup (optional)*
- *1 teaspoon of cinnamon (optional)*

Preparation:

1. In a pot, pour the milk and bring it to a boil over medium heat.
2. Procedure:
3. Add the oats to the pot and reduce the heat to medium-low. Let them simmer for about 5-7 minutes, stirring occasionally, until the oatmeal reaches the desired consistency.
4. Add the blueberries and continue to cook for another minute or two until they are heated through.
5. Remove the pot from the heat and pour the oatmeal into two individual bowls.
6. Top each bowl with chopped walnuts, and if desired, drizzle with honey or maple syrup and sprinkle with a pinch of cinnamon.

Nutritional Information (per serving):

Calories: 350

Protein: 10g

Fat: 12g

Carbohydrates: 53g

Fiber: 8g

Sugar: 10g

Glycemic Index (GI): The glycemic index of oatmeal is moderate, but the addition of fresh or frozen blueberries can help keep it relatively low. Cinnamon can also contribute to regulating the glycemic index. However, if you want to further reduce the GI, you can opt for low-GI oats or reduce the amount of blueberries and added sugars.

Greek Yogurt with Honey and Homemade Granola (for two)

- *Difficulty Level:* ☐☐
- *Prep Time: 10 minutes*
- *Cook Time: 20 minutes*
- *Cooking Levels: Easy*

Ingredients:

- *1 cup of Greek yogurt*
- *2 tablespoons of honey*
- *1/2 cup of homemade granola (see recipe below)*
- *Fresh berries (e.g., strawberries, blueberries) for topping*
- *Homemade Granola:*

- *1 cup rolled oats*
- *1/4 cup chopped nuts (e.g., almonds, walnuts)*
- *2 tablespoons honey or maple syrup*
- *1 tablespoon coconut oil*
- *1/2 teaspoon cinnamon*
- *A pinch of salt*
- *1/4 cup dried fruits (e.g., raisins, cranberries) (optional)*
-

Preparation:

1.   *Preheat your oven to 325°F (163°C).*
2.   *In a mixing bowl, combine the rolled oats, chopped nuts, honey or maple syrup, coconut oil, cinnamon, and a pinch of salt. Stir well to coat the oats and nuts evenly.*
3.   *Spread the mixture onto a baking sheet lined with parchment paper. Bake in the preheated oven for about 15-20 minutes, or until the granola turns golden brown, stirring occasionally to ensure even toasting.*
4.   *Once the granola is done, remove it from the oven and let it cool completely. If you'd like, add dried fruits like raisins or cranberries.*
5.   *To prepare the yogurt bowls, divide the Greek yogurt between two serving bowls.*
6.   *Drizzle 1 tablespoon of honey over each portion of yogurt.*
7.   *Sprinkle 1/4 cup of your homemade granola over each bowl of yogurt.*
8.   *Top with fresh berries or your choice of fruits.*
9.   *Serve and enjoy your Greek Yogurt with Honey and Homemade Granola!*

Nutritional Values (per serving):

Calories: 350

Protein: 12g

Fat: 14g

Carbohydrates: 48g

Fiber: 5g

Sugars: 24g

Glycemic Index (GI): The GI is low for this meal, as Greek yogurt and honey have relatively low GI values. The homemade granola may have a moderate GI due to the oats and honey, but its impact is balanced by the yogurt and berries.

Note: The provided granola recipe makes more than needed for this yogurt bowl. You can store the extra granola in an airtight container for future use.

Whole Wheat French Toast with Sliced Bananas

- *Cooking Skill:* □□
- *Preparation Time: 10 minutes*
- *Cooking Time: 10 minutes*
- *Cooking Level: Easy*

Ingredients:

- *2 slices of whole wheat bread*
- *2 eggs*
- *1/4 cup of milk (you can use regular milk or almond milk)*
- *1/2 teaspoon of vanilla extract*
- *1/2 teaspoon of ground cinnamon*
- *1 ripe banana, sliced*
- *1 tablespoon of honey or maple syrup (optional)*
- *Cooking spray or a small amount of butter for greasing the pan*

Instructions:

1. *In a shallow bowl, whisk together the eggs, milk, vanilla extract, and ground cinnamon.*

2. *Heat a non-stick skillet or griddle over medium heat and lightly grease it with cooking spray or butter.*

3. *Dip each slice of whole wheat bread into the egg mixture, ensuring it's coated on both sides.*

4. *Place the coated bread slices on the heated skillet and cook until they are golden brown on both sides, about 2-3 minutes per side.*

5. *Remove the French toast from the skillet and top with sliced bananas. Drizzle with honey or maple syrup if desired.*

Nutritional Information (per serving):

Calories: 300

Protein: 12g

Fat: 8g

Carbohydrates: 47g

Fiber: 6g

Sugar: 18g

Glycemic Index (GI): The whole wheat bread in this recipe has a lower GI compared to white bread, and the addition of bananas and honey or maple syrup may slightly raise the GI. However, it's still a relatively moderate GI dish. If you want to further reduce the GI, consider using sugar-free syrup or reducing the amount of sweetener.

Coconut Mango Chia Smoothie

- *Cooking Skill:* □
- *Preparation Time: 5 minutes*
- *Cooking Level: Easy*

Ingredients:

- *1 cup of unsweetened coconut milk*
- *1 cup of frozen mango chunks*
- *1 ripe banana*
- *1 tablespoon of chia seeds*
- *1 teaspoon of honey or agave syrup (optional, for added sweetness)*

Instructions:

1. In a blender, combine the unsweetened coconut milk, frozen mango chunks, ripe banana, and chia seeds.

2. If you prefer a sweeter smoothie, you can add honey or agave syrup to taste.

3. Blend until the mixture is smooth and all the ingredients are well combined.

4. Pour the smoothie into a glass and enjoy your refreshing coconut mango chia smoothie.

Nutritional Information (per serving):

Calories: 250

Protein: 4g

Fat: 8g

Carbohydrates: 42g

Fiber: 8g

Sugar: 26g

Glycemic Index (GI): This smoothie has a moderate GI due to the natural sugars in the mango and banana. The addition of chia seeds and coconut milk may help slow down the sugar absorption, making it a relatively healthy choice.

Whole Wheat Apple Cinnamon Muffins (for Two)

- **Difficulty Level: ☐☐**
- **Preparation Time: 15 minutes**
- **Baking Time: 20-25 minutes**
- **Baking Temperature: 350°F (180°C)**
- **Yields: 6 muffins**

Ingredients:

- 3/4 cup whole wheat flour
- 3/4 tsp baking powder
- 1/4 tsp baking soda
- 1/8 tsp salt
- 3/4 tsp ground cinnamon
- 2 tbsp unsalted butter, melted and cooled
- 2 tbsp honey or maple syrup
- 1/4 cup plain Greek yogurt
- 1 large egg
- 1/2 tsp vanilla extract
- 3/4 cup diced apples (about 1 medium-sized apple)
- 1/4 cup chopped walnuts (optional)

Instructions:

1. Preheat your oven to 350°F (180°C) and line a muffin tin with paper liners or grease the cups.

Dry Ingredients:

2. In a large bowl, whisk together the whole wheat flour, baking powder, baking soda, salt, and ground cinnamon. Set this dry mixture aside.

Wet Ingredients:

3. In another bowl, mix the melted butter, honey (or maple syrup), Greek yogurt, egg, and vanilla extract until well combined.

4. Pour the wet ingredients into the dry ingredients and stir until just combined. Do not overmix; it's okay if there are a few lumps.

5. Gently fold in the diced apples and chopped walnuts (if using).

Baking:

6. Divide the muffin batter evenly among the 6 muffin cups.

7. Bake in the preheated oven for 20-25 minutes or until a toothpick inserted into the center of a muffin comes out clean.

Cooling and Serving:

8. Allow the muffins to cool in the pan for a few minutes, then transfer them to a wire rack to cool completely.

9. Enjoy your whole wheat apple cinnamon muffins for two! These muffins can be stored in an airtight container for several days.

Nutritional Information (per muffin, for two servings):

Calories: 152

Protein: 4g

Fat: 6g

Carbohydrates: 24g

Fiber: 3g

Sugars: 12g

Glycemic Index (GI): The use of whole wheat flour and the natural sweetness from honey or maple syrup helps keep the GI relatively low. The fiber from apples and whole wheat flour further contributes to a slow and steady rise in blood sugar.

Whole Wheat Waffles with Strawberries and Yogurt (for Two)

- **Difficulty Level: □□□**
- **Preparation Time: 15 minutes**
- **Cooking Time: 10 minutes**
- **Cooking Appliance: Waffle Iron**
- **Yields: 4 waffles**

Ingredients:

- 1 cup whole wheat flour
- 1 1/2 tsp baking powder
- 1/2 tsp baking soda
- 1/4 tsp salt
- 1 cup buttermilk
- 1 large egg
- 2 tbsp honey or maple syrup
- 2 tbsp unsalted butter, melted and cooled
- 1/2 tsp vanilla extract
- 1 cup fresh strawberries, sliced
- 1/2 cup Greek yogurt
- Honey or maple syrup for drizzling (optional)

Preparation:

1. Preheat your waffle iron according to the manufacturer's instructions.

Dry Ingredients:

2. In a large bowl, whisk together the whole wheat flour, baking powder, baking soda, and salt.

Wet Ingredients:

3. In another bowl, whisk together the buttermilk, egg, honey (or maple syrup), melted butter, and vanilla extract.

4. Pour the wet ingredients into the bowl with the dry ingredients. Stir until just combined. Do not overmix; a few lumps are fine.

Cooking:

5. Grease the waffle iron with a bit of oil or non-stick cooking spray.

6. Pour an appropriate amount of waffle batter onto the preheated waffle iron (the amount may vary depending on the size of your waffle iron). Close the waffle iron and cook until the waffles are golden brown and crisp.

7. Carefully remove the waffles and set them aside. Continue cooking the remaining waffle batter.

Serving:

8. To serve, place two waffles on each plate.

9. Top the waffles with sliced strawberries and a dollop of Greek yogurt.

10. Drizzle honey or maple syrup on top, if desired.

11. Enjoy your whole wheat waffles with strawberries and yogurt!

Nutritional Information (per serving, 2 waffles each):

- Calories: 346
- Protein: 10g
- Fat: 10g
- Carbohydrates: 57g
- Fiber: 6g
- Sugars: 22g

- Glycemic Index (GI): The use of whole wheat flour and the addition of fresh strawberries

help keep the GI relatively low. The yogurt provides a source of protein and healthy fats to stabilize blood sugar levels. If you want to further reduce the GI, you can opt for a sugar-free syrup or skip the drizzle.

Yogurt Parfait with Strawberries and Cereal

- **Difficulty Level: ☐ ☐ **
- **Preparation Time: 10 minutes**
- **Yields: 2 servings**

Ingredients:
- 1 cup Greek yogurt
- 1 cup fresh strawberries, sliced
- 1/2 cup granola or your choice of whole-grain cereal
- 2 tablespoons honey (optional)
- Fresh mint leaves for garnish (optional)

Preparation:

1. In two serving glasses or bowls, start by adding a layer of Greek yogurt at the bottom.
2. Add a layer of sliced strawberries on top of the yogurt.
3. Sprinkle a layer of granola or whole-grain cereal over the strawberries.

Repeat the layers:

4. Add another layer of Greek yogurt.
5. Top it with more sliced strawberries.
6. Finish with another layer of granola or cereal.

Serving:

7. Drizzle honey over the top for added sweetness, if desired.

8. Garnish with fresh mint leaves for a pop of color and flavor (optional).

9. Serve immediately, or refrigerate for a short time if you prefer it chilled.

10. Enjoy your yogurt parfait with strawberries and cereal!

Nutritional Information (per serving):

- Calories: Approximately 300
- Protein: 15g
- Fat: 8g
- Carbohydrates: 45g
- Fiber: 5g
- Sugars: 20g
- Glycemic Index (GI): The glycemic index of this parfait is relatively low, thanks to the high-protein Greek yogurt, fresh strawberries, and whole-grain cereal. If you want to further reduce the GI, you can skip the honey or choose a sugar substitute.

Banana Crepes with Dark Chocolate

- **Difficulty Level: □□□**
- **Preparation Time: 20 minutes**
- **Cooking Time: 10 minutes**
- **Yields: 2 servings**

Ingredients:

For the Crepes:
- 1/2 cup whole wheat flour
- 1/2 cup low-fat milk (or plant-based milk)
- 2 large eggs
- 1 tablespoon honey (optional)
- 1/2 teaspoon vanilla extract
- A pinch of salt
- Cooking spray or a small amount of oil for greasing the pan

For the Filling:
- 2 ripe bananas, thinly sliced
- 2 ounces dark chocolate (70% cocoa or higher), finely chopped

Instructions:

Preparing the Crepe Batter:

1. In a blender or mixing bowl, combine the whole wheat flour, low-fat milk (or plant-based milk), eggs, honey (if using), vanilla extract, and a pinch of salt. Blend or whisk until you have a smooth batter.

Cooking the Crepes:

2. Heat a non-stick skillet over medium-high heat and lightly grease it with cooking spray or a small amount of oil.

3. Pour a small amount of crepe batter into the skillet, swirling it around to create a thin, even layer. Cook for about 1-2 minutes or until the edges start to lift.

4. Carefully flip the crepe and cook for an additional 1-2 minutes or until lightly golden. Repeat this process until you've used all the batter. You should have about 4-6 crepes, depending on the size of your skillet.

Assembling the Crepes:

5. Lay one crepe flat on a clean surface or a plate.

6. Place a few banana slices and a sprinkle of dark chocolate in the center of the crepe.

7. Fold the sides of the crepe over the filling to create a square or rectangular shape.

8. Repeat this process for each crepe.

Serving:

9. Place the filled crepes in the skillet for a quick warm-up, just enough to slightly melt the chocolate (about 1 minute on each side).

10. Arrange the crepes on serving plates.

11. You can drizzle a bit of honey or add a few more banana slices and a touch of dark chocolate on top if desired.

12. Serve your delightful banana crepes with dark chocolate while they're warm.

Nutritional Information (per serving, excluding extra toppings):

- Calories: Approximately 380

- Protein: 12g

- Fat: 11g

- Carbohydrates: 58g

- Fiber: 7g

- Sugars: 19g

- Glycemic Index (GI): The glycemic index of these crepes is moderate, primarily influenced by the whole wheat flour. The use of dark chocolate and ripe bananas complements the overall GI. If you want to lower the GI further, consider using a sugar substitute or reducing the amount of honey.

Carrot Cake for Breakfast

- **Difficulty Level: ☐☐**
- **Preparation Time: 15 minutes**
- **Cooking Time: 35 minutes**
- **Yields: 2 servings**

Ingredients:

For the Carrot Cake:
- 1 cup grated carrots
- 1/2 cup whole wheat flour
- 1/4 cup rolled oats
- 1/4 cup chopped walnuts or pecans
- 1/4 cup raisins
- 1/4 cup unsweetened applesauce
- 2 tablespoons honey or maple syrup
- 1 large egg
- 1/2 teaspoon baking powder
- 1/4 teaspoon baking soda
- 1/2 teaspoon ground cinnamon
- 1/4 teaspoon ground nutmeg
- A pinch of salt

For the Cream Cheese Topping (Optional):
- 1/4 cup low-fat cream cheese
- 1 tablespoon honey or maple syrup
- 1/2 teaspoon vanilla extract

Instructions:

Preparing the Carrot Cake:

1. Preheat your oven to 350°F (175°C) and grease a small baking dish or individual ramekins.

2. In a mixing bowl, combine the whole wheat flour, rolled oats, chopped nuts, raisins, baking powder, baking soda, ground cinnamon, ground nutmeg, and a pinch of salt. Mix well.

3. In another bowl, whisk together the grated carrots, unsweetened applesauce, honey (or maple syrup), and the egg.

4. Pour the wet ingredients into the dry ingredients and stir until just combined.

Baking the Carrot Cake:

5. Pour the carrot cake batter into the greased baking dish or ramekins.

6. Bake in the preheated oven for about 30-35 minutes, or until a toothpick inserted into the center comes out clean.

7. Remove the carrot cake from the oven and let it cool for a few minutes.

Preparing the Cream Cheese Topping (Optional):

8. In a small bowl, whisk together the low-fat cream cheese, honey (or maple syrup), and vanilla extract until you have a smooth and sweet topping.

Serving:

9. Once the carrot cake has cooled slightly, you can either serve it as is or top it with the cream cheese topping.

10. Slice the carrot cake into portions and enjoy a delightful and healthy carrot cake for breakfast!

Nutritional Information (per serving, with cream cheese topping):

Calories: Approximately 350 (without topping: about 280)

Protein: 8g (without topping: about 7g)

Fat: 11g (without topping: about 8g)

Carbohydrates: 55g (without topping: about 46g)

Fiber: 7g (without topping: about 6g)

Sugars: 29g (without topping: about 22g)

Glycemic Index (GI): The glycemic index of this carrot cake is relatively moderate due to the whole wheat flour and natural sweeteners.

SAVORY OPTIONS:

Scrambled Eggs with Spinach and Sun-Dried Tomatoes

- Difficulty Level: ☐☐
- Preparation Time: 10 minutes
- Cooking Time: 10 minutes
- Cooking Level: Easy

Ingredients:

- 4 large eggs
- 1/4 cup milk
- 1 cup fresh spinach, chopped
- 1/4 cup sun-dried tomatoes, chopped
- 1/4 cup grated Parmesan cheese
- Salt and pepper to taste
- 1 tablespoon olive oil
-

Instructions:

1. In a bowl, whisk together the eggs, milk, and a pinch of salt and pepper.

2. Heat olive oil in a non-stick skillet over medium heat.

3. Add the chopped spinach and sun-dried tomatoes to the skillet. Sauté for about 2-3 minutes or until the spinach wilts and the tomatoes become slightly tender.

4. Pour the egg mixture over the spinach and tomatoes. Let it sit undisturbed for a minute or two until the edges start to set.

5. Gently scramble the eggs with a spatula, folding them over as they cook.

6. When the eggs are almost set but still slightly creamy, sprinkle the grated Parmesan cheese over the top.

7. Continue cooking and folding until the eggs are fully cooked but still moist.

8. Season with additional salt and pepper to taste if needed.

9. Serve the scrambled eggs hot, garnished with extra Parmesan cheese if desired.

Nutritional Values (per serving):

Calories: 300

Protein: 20g

Fat: 19g

Carbohydrates: 13g

Fiber: 3g

Sugars: 6g

Glycemic Index (GI): The glycemic index of this dish is relatively low. Eggs, spinach, and sun-dried tomatoes have minimal impact on blood sugar levels, while milk and Parmesan cheese have minimal to low GI.

Overall, this savory scrambled eggs recipe should have a low to moderate glycemic index, making it a good choice for those looking to manage their blood sugar levels. However, individual responses to food can vary, so it's always a good idea for individuals with specific dietary concerns to monitor their blood sugar levels and adjust their diet accordingly.

Avocado Toast with Sunny-Side-Up Eggs

- Difficulty Level: ☐☐
- Preparation Time: 10 minutes
- Cooking Time: 10 minutes
- Cooking Level: Easy

Ingredients:

- 2 slices of whole-grain bread
- 1 ripe avocado
- 2 large eggs
- Salt and pepper to taste
- Red pepper flakes (optional, for added spice)
- Fresh chives or parsley for garnish (optional)

Instructions:

1. Toast the slices of whole-grain bread until they reach your desired level of crispiness.

2. While the bread is toasting, cut the ripe avocado in half, remove the pit, and scoop the flesh into a bowl. Mash it with a fork and season with a pinch of salt and pepper. You can also add a dash of red pepper flakes if you like a little heat.

3. In a non-stick skillet, heat a small amount of oil over medium-low heat.

4. Crack each egg into the skillet carefully, ensuring the yolks remain intact. Season each egg with a pinch of salt and pepper.

5. Cover the skillet with a lid and cook the eggs until the whites are set, but the yolks are still runny. This typically takes about 2-3 minutes. If you prefer fully cooked yolks, cook them a bit longer.

6. Once the eggs are ready, remove the skillet from heat.

7. Spread the mashed avocado evenly on the toasted bread slices.

8. Carefully transfer the sunny-side-up eggs on top of the avocado-covered toast.

9. Garnish with fresh chives or parsley if desired.

10. Season with additional salt, pepper, or red pepper flakes according to your taste.

11. Serve your avocado toast with sunny-side-up eggs immediately while it's still warm.

Nutritional Values (for the entire recipe, which serves 2):

Calories: 420

Protein: 16g

Fat: 27g

Carbohydrates: 31g

Fiber: 12g

Sugars: 3g

Glycemic Index (GI): This meal has a low glycemic index. Whole-grain bread and avocado have minimal impact on blood sugar, while eggs have a GI of zero. It's a balanced and nutritious option suitable for those aiming to maintain steady blood sugar levels. However, individual responses to food can vary, so always monitor your blood sugar levels and adjust your diet as needed based on your specific health requirements.

Mixed Vegetable Frittata

- Difficulty Level: ☐☐
- Preparation Time: 15 minutes
- Cooking Time: 20 minutes
- Cooking Level: Moderate

Ingredients:

- 4 large eggs
- 1/4 cup milk
- 1/2 cup bell peppers, diced (use a mix of red, green, and yellow for color)
- 1/2 cup zucchini, diced
- 1/2 cup cherry tomatoes, halved
- 1/4 cup red onion, finely chopped
- 1/4 cup fresh spinach, chopped
- 1/4 cup grated Parmesan cheese
- 2 tablespoons olive oil
- Salt and pepper to taste
- Fresh basil or parsley for garnish (optional)

Instructions:

1. Preheat your oven's broiler.

2. In a medium-sized bowl, whisk together the eggs, milk, and grated Parmesan cheese. Season the mixture with a pinch of salt and pepper.

3. Heat the olive oil in an ovenproof skillet (preferably non-stick) over medium heat.

4. Add the chopped red onion and sauté for about 2-3 minutes until they become translucent.

5. Add the diced bell peppers and zucchini to the skillet. Cook for another 4-5 minutes, or until they start to soften.

6. Stir in the halved cherry tomatoes and chopped spinach, then cook for an additional 2-3 minutes, or until the spinach wilts and the tomatoes begin to soften.

7. Pour the egg and cheese mixture over the sautéed vegetables in the skillet. Stir gently to distribute the veggies evenly.

8. Allow the frittata to cook without stirring for about 3-4 minutes, or until the edges begin to set.

9. Transfer the skillet to the preheated broiler and broil for another 3-4 minutes until the frittata is fully set and slightly golden on top.

10. Remove the skillet from the oven (remember to use oven mitts as the handle will be hot).

11. Run a spatula around the edges to loosen the frittata, then slide it onto a plate or serving platter.

12. Garnish with fresh basil or parsley if desired.

13. Slice the frittata into wedges and serve.

14. Enjoy your mixed vegetable frittata as a delicious and nutritious meal.

Nutritional Values (for the entire frittata):

Calories: 450
Protein: 22g
Fat: 34g
Carbohydrates: 18g
Fiber: 4g
Sugars: 9g

Note: The glycemic index of this frittata is low, as it mainly consists of non-starchy vegetables and eggs. It's a balanced and healthy option for maintaining stable blood sugar levels. However, always monitor your individual responses to food and make adjustments as necessary based on your specific dietary needs.

Black Bean Burrito with Tomato Salsa

- Difficulty Level: ☐☐
- Preparation Time: 20 minutes
- Cooking Time: 10 minutes
- Cooking Level: Easy

Ingredients:

For the Black Bean Filling:
- 1 can (15 oz) of black beans, drained and rinsed
- 1/2 cup diced onion
- 1 clove garlic, minced
- 1 teaspoon ground cumin
- 1 teaspoon chili powder
- Salt and pepper to taste
- 1 tablespoon olive oil

For the Tomato Salsa:
- 1 cup diced tomatoes
- 1/4 cup diced red onion
- 1/4 cup chopped fresh cilantro

- Juice of 1 lime
- Salt and pepper to taste

For Assembling:
- 2 large whole-grain tortillas
- 1 cup cooked brown rice
- 1 cup shredded lettuce
- 1/2 cup shredded cheddar cheese (optional)
- Greek yogurt or sour cream for garnish (optional)
- Sliced avocado for garnish (optional)

Instructions:

Black Bean Filling:

1. In a skillet, heat the olive oil over medium heat. Add the diced onion and sauté for 2-3 minutes until it becomes translucent.

2. Add the minced garlic and sauté for an additional 30 seconds until fragrant.

3. Stir in the drained black beans, cumin, chili powder, salt, and pepper. Cook for about 5-7 minutes until the beans are heated through and the flavors meld. Mash some of the beans with a fork for a creamier texture.

Tomato Salsa:

1. In a bowl, combine the diced tomatoes, red onion, chopped cilantro, lime juice, salt, and pepper. Mix well and set aside.

Assembling the Burrito:

1. Warm the whole-grain tortillas in a dry skillet or microwave for a few seconds to make them more pliable.

2. Lay each tortilla flat and add 1/2 cup of cooked brown rice in the center.

3. Top the rice with half of the black bean filling, followed by shredded lettuce and cheddar cheese, if desired.

4. Spoon tomato salsa on top of the filling.

5. Optionally, add a dollop of Greek yogurt or sour cream and some sliced avocado.

6. Fold the sides of the tortilla in and then roll it up, tucking the sides as you go to create a burrito.

7. Serve the black bean burrito with tomato salsa immediately and enjoy!

Nutritional Values (per burrito, excluding optional toppings):

Calories: 400
Protein: 14g
Fat: 8g
Carbohydrates: 70g
Fiber: 11g
Sugars: 5g

Note: This black bean burrito is a nutritious and satisfying meal with a low to moderate glycemic index, thanks to whole-grain tortillas, brown rice, and black beans. It provides complex carbohydrates and plant-based proteins for sustained energy. Customize it with your choice of optional toppings to suit your taste.

Whole Wheat Peanut Butter and Banana Toast

- Difficulty Level: ☐
- Preparation Time: 5 minutes
- Cooking Level: Easy

Ingredients:

- 2 slices of whole wheat bread
- 2-3 tablespoons natural peanut butter
- 1-2 ripe bananas, sliced
- Honey or a drizzle of maple syrup (optional)
- Chia seeds (optional)
- Cinnamon powder (optional)

Instructions:

1. Toast the whole wheat bread slices to your desired level of crispiness.

2. While the toast is still warm, spread 1-1.5 tablespoons of natural peanut butter on each slice.

3. Arrange the banana slices on top of the peanut butter.

4. Optionally, drizzle honey or maple syrup for a touch of sweetness.

5. If desired, sprinkle some chia seeds for added texture and nutrition.

6. A pinch of cinnamon powder can be added for extra flavor.

7. Place the two slices of toast together to make a sandwich or enjoy them open-faced.

8. Serve your whole wheat peanut butter and banana toast immediately, and savor this delicious and nutritious breakfast or snack.

Nutritional Values (for two slices):

Calories: Approximately 400
Protein: 10g
Fat: 13g
Carbohydrates: 65g
Fiber: 8g
Sugars: 19g

Note: This whole wheat peanut butter and banana toast provides a good balance of protein, healthy fats, and complex carbohydrates. The use of whole wheat bread and natural peanut butter ensures a moderate glycemic index. You can customize it with optional ingredients like honey, chia seeds, or cinnamon to suit your preferences.

Baked Sweet Potatoes with Eggs and Spinach

- Difficulty Level: ☐☐
- Preparation Time: 15 minutes
- Cooking Level: Intermediate

Ingredients:

- 2 medium-sized sweet potatoes
- 4 large eggs

- 2 cups fresh spinach, chopped
- 1/2 red onion, finely chopped
- 2 cloves garlic, minced
- 1 tablespoon olive oil
- 1/2 teaspoon paprika
- Salt and pepper to taste
- Fresh parsley for garnish (optional)

Instructions:

1. Preheat your oven to 400°F (200°C).

2. Wash and scrub the sweet potatoes thoroughly. Prick them several times with a fork.

3. Place the sweet potatoes on a baking sheet and bake for about 45-60 minutes or until they are tender. The exact time may vary depending on their size. You can check for doneness by inserting a fork into the sweet potatoes; it should go in easily.

4. While the sweet potatoes are baking, heat the olive oil in a large skillet over medium heat.

5. Add the chopped onion and minced garlic to the skillet. Sauté for about 2-3 minutes until the onions become translucent.

6. Add the chopped spinach to the skillet and sauté for another 2-3 minutes until it wilts. Season with salt, pepper, and paprika.

7. Create four wells in the spinach mixture and crack an egg into each well.

8. Cover the skillet and cook for about 4-6 minutes, or until the egg whites are set but the yolks are still slightly runny. If you prefer fully cooked yolks, cook for a few more minutes.

9. Once the sweet potatoes are done, remove them from the oven. Cut a slit lengthwise in each potato and fluff the insides with a fork.

10. Place one baked sweet potato on each plate and top them with the spinach and eggs.

11. Garnish with fresh parsley if desired, and serve your delicious baked sweet potatoes with eggs and spinach immediately.

Nutritional Values (per serving):

Calories: Approximately 320

Protein: 14g

Fat: 12g

Carbohydrates: 40g

Fiber: 7g

Sugars: 8g

Note: This dish combines the goodness of sweet potatoes, eggs, and spinach to provide a healthy and filling meal. The eggs offer protein, while sweet potatoes provide complex carbs and fiber. Spinach adds essential vitamins and minerals. Adjust the cooking time for the eggs to achieve your preferred level of doneness.

Whole Wheat Tortilla with Cheese and Ham

- Difficulty Level: ☐
- Preparation Time: 10 minutes
- Cooking Level: Easy

Ingredients:

- 2 whole wheat tortillas

- 2-4 slices of lean ham
- 1/2 cup shredded cheddar cheese
- 1/4 cup sliced bell peppers (red, green, or yellow, based on preference)
- 1/4 cup sliced red onion
- Cooking spray or a small amount of olive oil for toasting

Instructions:

1. Lay out one whole wheat tortilla on a clean surface or plate.

2. Sprinkle half of the shredded cheddar cheese evenly over half of the tortilla.

3. Layer the ham slices, bell peppers, and red onions over the cheese.

4. Sprinkle the remaining cheddar cheese on top.

5. Fold the other half of the tortilla over the ingredients, creating a half-moon shape.

6. Heat a non-stick skillet over medium heat and lightly grease it with cooking spray or a small amount of olive oil.

7. Place the folded tortilla in the skillet and cook for about 2-3 minutes on each side or until it's golden brown and the cheese is melted.

8. Remove the tortilla from the skillet and let it cool for a minute.

9. Using a sharp knife, cut the tortilla in half to create two delicious cheese and ham quesadillas.

10. Serve your whole wheat tortilla with cheese and ham while it's still warm, and enjoy!

Nutritional Values (per serving - 1 quesadilla):

Calories: Approximately 280

Protein: 18g

Fat: 10g

Carbohydrates: 26g

Fiber: 4g

Sugars: 4g

Note: This whole wheat tortilla with cheese and ham is a quick and satisfying meal. The whole wheat tortilla provides fiber, and you can customize the vegetables to your liking. It's a great option for a fast and healthy lunch or dinner.

The glycemic index (GI) for this whole wheat tortilla with cheese and ham is relatively moderate. The whole wheat tortilla contains complex carbohydrates that are digested more slowly, leading to a gradual increase in blood sugar levels. The inclusion of vegetables, such as bell peppers and onions, further contributes to stabilizing blood sugar levels. However, it's essential to note that individual responses to the GI can vary. If you have specific concerns about blood sugar, it's a good idea to monitor your levels and consult with a healthcare professional for personalized dietary advice.

Coffee Banana Almond Smoothie

- *Difficulty Level:* ☐☐
- *Preparation Time: 5 minutes*
- *Cooking Time: 0 minutes*
- *Cooking Level: Easy*

Ingredients:

- 1 ripe banana
- 1 cup of cold brewed coffee
- 1/4 cup of unsalted almonds
- 1 cup of low-fat Greek yogurt
- 1 tablespoon of honey (optional)
- Ice cubes (optional)
- Instructions:

1. Peel the ripe banana and break it into a few pieces.

2. In a blender, combine the banana pieces, cold brewed coffee, unsalted almonds, and low-fat Greek yogurt.

3. If you prefer a sweeter smoothie, add a tablespoon of honey to the blender.

4. Optionally, you can include a few ice cubes for a colder and thicker consistency.

5. Blend all the ingredients until the smoothie is well mixed and reaches your desired consistency.

Enjoy your Coffee Banana Almond Smoothie as a refreshing and energizing drink!

Nutritional Values (per serving):

Calories: 250

Protein: 10g

Fat: 7g

Carbohydrates: 40g

Fiber: 5g

Sugar: 22g

Glycemic Index (GI): The glycemic index of this smoothie is relatively low due to the presence of fiber-rich ingredients like banana and almonds. The cold brewed coffee and low-fat Greek yogurt provide a source of protein and complex carbohydrates, helping to regulate blood sugar levels. However, if you have specific concerns about blood sugar, it's advisable to monitor your levels and consult with a healthcare professional for personalized dietary guidance.

CEREAL-BASED OPTIONS:

Berry Yogurt Muesli

- Difficulty Level: ☐
- Preparation Time: 10 minutes
- Cooking Time: 0 minutes
- Cooking Level: Easy

Ingredients:

- 1 cup of rolled oats
- 1 cup of low-fat yogurt
- 1/2 cup of mixed berries (strawberries, blueberries, raspberries)
- 1 tablespoon of honey or maple syrup (optional)
- 1/4 cup of chopped nuts (e.g., almonds, walnuts)

Instructions:

1. In a mixing bowl, combine rolled oats, low-fat yogurt, and mixed berries. Mix well.

2. If you prefer a sweeter muesli, add a tablespoon of honey or maple syrup to the mixture. Stir until evenly distributed.

3. Top your muesli with chopped nuts. You can choose your favorite, such as almonds, walnuts, or any other nut you prefer.

4. Allow the muesli to sit for a few minutes to let the flavors meld together. You can also refrigerate it for a while if you like it chilled.

5. Serve your Berry Yogurt Muesli in a bowl or glass, and enjoy a healthy and refreshing breakfast.

Nutritional Values (per serving):

Calories: 350

Protein: 10g

Fat: 12g

Carbohydrates: 50g

Fiber: 7g

Sugar: 20g

Glycemic Index (GI): This muesli has a low glycemic index, mainly due to the complex carbohydrates from oats and the fiber-rich berries. The addition of nuts and yogurt provides healthy fats and protein, further stabilizing blood sugar levels. If you need to manage your blood sugar, consult a healthcare professional for personalized dietary advice.

Quinoa and Fresh Fruit Porridge

- *Difficulty Level:* ☐
- *Preparation Time: 15 minutes*
- *Cooking Time: 15 minutes*
- *Cooking Level: Easy*

Ingredients:

- *1/2 cup quinoa*
- *1 cup water*
- *1 cup milk (regular, almond, or soy)*
- *1/2 teaspoon vanilla extract*
- *2 cups mixed fresh fruit (e.g., berries, sliced banana, diced apple)*
- *2 tablespoons honey or maple syrup (optional)*
- *A pinch of cinnamon (optional)*

Instructions:

Preparation:

1. Rinse the quinoa under cold running water in a fine-mesh strainer.

2. In a medium-sized saucepan, combine the rinsed quinoa and water. Bring to a boil over medium-high heat.

3. Reduce the heat to low, cover, and simmer for about 15 minutes, or until the quinoa has absorbed all the water and is cooked. It should have a slightly translucent outer ring when done.

4. Fluff the quinoa with a fork and let it cool slightly.

Porridge Assembly:

1. In a separate saucepan, heat the milk over low to medium heat until it's hot but not boiling.

2. Stir in the cooked quinoa and vanilla extract. Continue to cook, stirring frequently, until the mixture thickens and reaches your desired porridge consistency.

3. Once the porridge is ready, remove it from the heat.

4. Divide the porridge into two bowls.

5. Top each bowl with a generous amount of mixed fresh fruit, such as berries, sliced banana, and diced apple.

6. Optionally, drizzle honey or maple syrup over the fruit for added sweetness.

7. A pinch of cinnamon can be sprinkled on top if desired.

8. Serve your Quinoa and Fresh Fruit Porridge hot and enjoy a nutritious and delicious breakfast.

Nutritional Values (per serving):

Calories: 350

Protein: 9g

Fat: 4g

Carbohydrates: 73g

Fiber: 8g

Sugar: 20g

Glycemic Index (GI): This porridge has a moderate glycemic index due to the presence of quinoa and mixed fruits. It can be a suitable breakfast choice for many, but individual responses may vary depending on the type and amount of fruit used.

Whole Grain Cereal with Almond Milk and Honey

- Difficulty Level: ☐
- Preparation Time: 5 minutes
- Cooking Time: 0 minutes
- Cooking Level: Easy

Ingredients:

- 1 cup whole grain cereal
- 2 cups almond milk (or milk of your choice)
- 1-2 tablespoons honey (adjust to taste)

Instructions:

1. In a cereal bowl, measure out one cup of whole grain cereal.

2. Pour two cups of almond milk (or your preferred type of milk) over the cereal.

3. Drizzle one to two tablespoons of honey over the cereal and milk. Adjust the amount of honey to your desired level of sweetness.

4. Stir the cereal, milk, and honey together, making sure the honey is well incorporated.

5. Let the cereal sit for a minute or two to allow the flavors to meld together and for the cereal to absorb some of the milk.

6. Enjoy your Whole Grain Cereal with Almond Milk and Honey as a quick and nutritious breakfast.

Nutritional Values (per serving):

Calories: 300

Protein: 8g

Fat: 5g

Carbohydrates: 60g

Fiber: 8g

Sugar: 18g

Glycemic Index (GI): The glycemic index of this breakfast is generally low because whole grain cereals release sugar slowly into the bloodstream. The honey may slightly raise the GI, but overall, it's still a relatively healthy and low-GI option.

Homemade Granola with Nuts and Seeds

- Difficulty Level: ☐☐

- *Preparation Time: 10 minutes*
- *Cooking Time: 25-30 minutes*
- *Cooking Level: Intermediate*

Ingredients:

- *2 cups rolled oats*
- *1/2 cup chopped nuts (such as almonds, walnuts, or pecans)*
- *1/4 cup pumpkin seeds*
- *1/4 cup sunflower seeds*
- *2 tablespoons flaxseeds*
- *1/2 teaspoon ground cinnamon*
- *1/4 teaspoon salt*
- *1/4 cup honey or maple syrup*
- *1/4 cup coconut oil, melted*
- *1/2 teaspoon vanilla extract*
- *1/2 cup dried fruit (such as raisins, cranberries, or apricots)*

Instructions:

1. Preheat your oven to 300°F (150°C) and line a baking sheet with parchment paper.

2. In a large mixing bowl, combine the rolled oats, chopped nuts, pumpkin seeds, sunflower seeds, flaxseeds, ground cinnamon, and salt.

3. In a separate microwave-safe bowl, heat the honey (or maple syrup), coconut oil, and vanilla extract until they're warm and easy to mix, about 20-30 seconds in the microwave.

4. Pour the warm honey mixture over the dry ingredients and stir well until everything is evenly coated.

5. Spread the granola mixture onto the prepared baking sheet in an even layer.

6. Bake in the preheated oven for 25-30 minutes, or until the granola is golden brown, stirring it gently every 10 minutes to ensure even cooking.

7. Remove the granola from the oven and let it cool on the baking sheet. It will become crunchier as it cools.

8. Once the granola has cooled, stir in the dried fruit.

9. Transfer your homemade granola to an airtight container for storage. Enjoy it with yogurt, milk, or as a snack.

Nutritional Values (per serving - approximately 1/4 cup):

Calories: 120

Protein: 3g

Fat: 7g

Carbohydrates: 12g

Fiber: 2g

Sugar: 6g

Glycemic Index (GI): The glycemic index of homemade granola can vary depending on the ingredients used. Whole oats and nuts tend to have a lower GI, while added sugars like honey or maple syrup can slightly increase it. Overall, it's a moderate-GI option when consumed in reasonable portions.

Whole Grain Risotto with Avocado and Sun-Dried Tomatoes

- *Difficulty Level: □□*
- *Preparation Time: 10 minutes*
- *Cooking Time: 40 minutes*
- *Cooking Level: Intermediate*

Ingredients:

- 1 cup whole grain rice (such as brown rice or whole grain Arborio rice)
- 2 1/2 cups vegetable or chicken broth (low-sodium)
- 1 ripe avocado, peeled and diced
- 1/4 cup sun-dried tomatoes, chopped
- 1 small onion, finely chopped
- 2 cloves garlic, minced
- 2 tablespoons olive oil
- 1/4 cup white wine (optional)
- 1/4 cup grated Parmesan cheese (optional)
- Salt and black pepper to taste
- Fresh basil leaves for garnish

Instructions:

1. In a medium saucepan, heat the vegetable or chicken broth and keep it warm over low heat. You'll use this to gradually add to the rice.

2. In a large skillet or saucepan, heat the olive oil over medium heat. Add the chopped onion and sauté until it becomes translucent, about 2-3 minutes.

3. Add the minced garlic and sauté for another 30 seconds until fragrant.

4. Add the whole grain rice to the skillet and stir to coat the rice with the oil, onions, and garlic. Cook for 1-2 minutes, or until the rice is lightly toasted.

5. If you're using white wine, pour it into the skillet and stir until it's mostly absorbed.

6. Begin adding the warm broth to the rice, one ladleful at a time. Stir continuously and allow the liquid to be absorbed before adding more.

Continue this process until the rice is tender and has a creamy consistency. This should take about 30-35 minutes.

7. Add the diced avocado and chopped sun-dried tomatoes to the risotto during the last 5 minutes of cooking. Stir gently to incorporate them without mashing the avocado.

8. If desired, stir in the grated Parmesan cheese until it's melted into the risotto. Season with salt and black pepper to taste.

9. Serve the whole grain risotto immediately, garnished with fresh basil leaves.

Nutritional Values (per serving):

Calories: 300

Protein: 6g

Fat: 10g

Carbohydrates: 45g

Fiber: 7g

Sugar: 2g

Glycemic Index (GI): Whole grain rice has a lower glycemic index compared to white rice, making this whole grain risotto a better choice for blood sugar control. Avocado and sun-dried tomatoes are low-GI ingredients, further enhancing the overall glycemic response. However, the addition of white wine or Parmesan cheese can slightly affect the GI.

Baked Oatmeal with Apples and Cinnamon

- Difficulty Level: ☐☐
- Preparation Time: 15 minutes
- Cooking Time: 40 minutes
- Cooking Level: Intermediate

Ingredients:

- 2 cups old-fashioned oats
- 1/2 cup chopped nuts (such as almonds or walnuts)
- 1 teaspoon baking powder
- 2 teaspoons ground cinnamon
- 1/4 teaspoon salt
- 2 cups milk (regular or almond milk)
- 1/4 cup pure maple syrup or honey
- 2 large eggs
- 2 tablespoons melted butter or coconut oil
- 2 teaspoons pure vanilla extract
- 2 medium apples, peeled, cored, and diced
- Additional apple slices, nuts, and a drizzle of maple syrup for garnish (optional)

Instructions:

1. Preheat your oven to 350°F (175°C). Grease a baking dish (about 8x8 inches) with butter or non-stick cooking spray.

2. In a large mixing bowl, combine the old-fashioned oats, chopped nuts, baking powder, ground cinnamon, and salt.

3. In another bowl, whisk together the milk, pure maple syrup or honey, eggs, melted butter or coconut oil, and pure vanilla extract.

4. Pour the wet ingredients into the bowl with the dry ingredients and mix until everything is well combined.

5. Add the diced apples and gently fold them into the oat mixture.

6. Pour the mixture into the greased baking dish and spread it out evenly.

7. If desired, place additional apple slices on top and sprinkle some extra chopped nuts over the surface.

8. Bake in the preheated oven for about 35-40 minutes or until the oatmeal is set and the top is golden brown.

9. Remove the baked oatmeal from the oven and allow it to cool for a few minutes before serving. You can drizzle a bit of maple syrup over the top for extra sweetness if you like.

10. Serve warm as is or with a dollop of Greek yogurt or a splash of milk.

Nutritional Values (per serving):

Calories: 300
Protein: 8g
Fat: 12g
Carbohydrates: 42g
Fiber: 6g
Sugar: 20g

Glycemic Index (GI): The GI of this baked oatmeal is moderate due to the presence of oats and apples, which have lower GI values. The use of pure maple syrup or honey may affect the GI slightly, so be mindful if you have specific dietary concerns.

Buckwheat Pancakes with Blueberries

- Difficulty Level: ☐☐
- Preparation Time: 10 minutes
- Cooking Time: 15 minutes

- Cooking Level: Intermediate

Ingredients:

- 1 cup buckwheat flour
- 2 tablespoons sugar
- 1 teaspoon baking powder
- 1/2 teaspoon baking soda
- 1/4 teaspoon salt
- 1 cup buttermilk (or a mixture of yogurt and water)
- 1 large egg
- 2 tablespoons melted butter
- 1/2 cup blueberries (fresh or frozen)
- Honey or maple syrup for drizzling (optional)

Instructions:

1. In a bowl, combine the buckwheat flour, sugar, baking powder, baking soda, and salt.

2. In a separate bowl, whisk together the buttermilk, egg, and melted butter.

3. Pour the wet mixture into the bowl with the dry ingredients and mix until just combined. Be careful not to overmix; a few lumps are okay.

4. Gently fold in the blueberries.

5. Heat a non-stick skillet or griddle over medium heat. Lightly grease it with butter or cooking spray.

6. Pour a ladleful of pancake batter onto the skillet for each pancake. Cook until you see bubbles forming on the surface, then flip and cook until the other side is golden brown. This usually takes about 2-3 minutes per side.

7. Continue this process until all the batter is used.

8. Serve the buckwheat pancakes hot, with a drizzle of honey or maple syrup if you like.

Nutritional Values (per serving):

Calories: 200

Protein: 6g

Fat: 6g

Carbohydrates: 32g

Fiber: 3g

Sugar: 6g

Glycemic Index (GI): Buckwheat flour has a lower glycemic index compared to regular wheat flour, which helps keep the GI of these pancakes relatively moderate. Blueberries are also a low-GI fruit. If you opt for honey or maple syrup, be aware that they can add some sweetness and potentially raise the GI slightly.

Green Smoothie with Spinach, Banana, and Avocado

- Difficulty Level: ☐
- Preparation Time: 5 minutes
- Cooking Time: 0 minutes
- Cooking Level: Easy

Ingredients:

- 1 cup fresh spinach leaves
- 1 ripe banana
- 1/2 ripe avocado
- 1 cup almond milk (or any milk of your choice)
- 1 tablespoon honey (optional, for sweetness)
- 1/2 cup ice cubes

Instructions:

1. Place the fresh spinach, ripe banana, ripe avocado, almond milk, and honey (if desired) in a blender.

2. Add the ice cubes to the blender to give your smoothie a refreshing chill.

3. Blend all the ingredients until the mixture is smooth and creamy. If it's too thick, you can add a bit more almond milk to reach your desired consistency.

4. Taste the smoothie and adjust the sweetness by adding more honey if needed.

5. Pour the green smoothie into a glass and serve immediately. Enjoy!

Nutritional Values (per serving):

Calories: 280

Protein: 4g

Fat: 15g

Carbohydrates: 37g

Fiber: 8g

Sugar: 19g

Glycemic Index (GI): This smoothie has a low glycemic index due to its high fiber content, especially from spinach, banana, and avocado. It's a great option for those looking to maintain stable blood sugar levels.

Whole Wheat Crepes with Ham and Cheese

- *Difficulty Level: ☐☐*
- *Preparation Time: 15 minutes*
- *Cooking Time: 20 minutes*
- *Cooking Level: Intermediate*

Ingredients:

For the Crepes:

- *1 cup whole wheat flour*
- *2 eggs*
- *1 cup milk*
- *1/2 cup water*
- *2 tablespoons melted butter*
- *1/4 teaspoon salt*

For the Filling:

- *4 slices of ham*
- *1 cup shredded cheese (e.g., Swiss, Gruyère, or cheddar)*
- *Fresh parsley, chopped, for garnish (optional)*

Instructions:

1. In a blender, combine the whole wheat flour, eggs, milk, water, melted butter, and salt. Blend until the batter is smooth. Allow the batter to rest for at least 30 minutes in the refrigerator to let the gluten relax.

2. Heat a non-stick skillet over medium-high heat and lightly grease it with a small amount of butter or cooking spray.

3. Pour a small amount of crepe batter into the center of the skillet and quickly tilt the pan in all directions so the batter covers the bottom evenly. Cook for about 1-2 minutes until the edges of the crepe start to lift from the pan. Flip the crepe and cook for an additional 1-2 minutes until lightly golden. Repeat this process with the remaining batter, stacking the cooked crepes on a plate.

4. Lay out a crepe, place a slice of ham on top, and sprinkle shredded cheese over the ham. Fold the crepe in half, then fold it in half again to form a triangle. Repeat with the remaining crepes.

5. Heat the filled crepes in the skillet or in the oven until the cheese is melted and the ham is heated through.

6. Garnish with chopped fresh parsley if desired and serve immediately.

Enjoy your whole wheat crepes with ham and cheese!

Nutritional Values (per serving, 2 crepes):

Calories: 350

Protein: 16g

Fat: 16g

Carbohydrates: 34g

Fiber: 4g

Sugar: 2g

Glycemic Index (GI): Whole wheat crepes have a lower GI compared to traditional white flour crepes, making them a better choice for blood sugar control. The ham and cheese in this recipe don't significantly affect the GI.

Oatmeal with Nuts and Dried Fruits

- Difficulty Level: ☐
- Preparation Time: 10 minutes
- Cooking Time: 5 minutes
- Cooking Level: Easy

Ingredients:

- 1 cup rolled oats
- 2 cups milk (you can choose regular milk, almond milk, or soy milk)
- 1/4 cup mixed nuts (e.g., almonds, walnuts, or pecans), chopped
- 1/4 cup dried fruits (e.g., raisins, cranberries, or apricots), chopped
- 1 tablespoon honey or maple syrup (optional)
- 1/2 teaspoon ground cinnamon (optional)

Instructions:

Preparation:

1. In a small bowl, combine the chopped nuts and dried fruits. Set aside to use as a topping for the oatmeal.

2. If you prefer your oatmeal sweetened, you can mix the honey or maple syrup with your choice of milk. Alternatively, you can drizzle it on top after cooking the oatmeal.

Cooking:

1. In a saucepan, add the rolled oats and milk. If using sweetener, add it now as well.

2. Place the saucepan over medium heat and bring the mixture to a gentle simmer. Stir occasionally to prevent sticking.

3. Let the oatmeal simmer for about 3-5 minutes, or until it reaches your desired thickness. If you prefer a thinner consistency, you can add a little extra milk.

4. Once the oatmeal is cooked to your liking, remove it from the heat and let it sit for a minute to cool slightly.

Serving:

1. Divide the oatmeal into two bowls.

2. Top the oatmeal with the mixed nuts and dried fruits.

3. If desired, sprinkle a pinch of ground cinnamon on each serving.

4. Serve your delicious oatmeal with nuts and dried fruits warm.

Enjoy your nutritious and comforting oatmeal with nuts and dried fruits!

Nutritional Values (per serving):

Calories: 350
Protein: 10g
Fat: 10g
Carbohydrates: 56g
Fiber: 6g
Sugar: 24g

Glycemic Index (GI): The oatmeal in this recipe has a moderate GI, but it can vary depending on the type of oats used. The added dried fruits may slightly increase the GI due to their natural sugars.

FRUIT-BASED OPTIONS:

Grilled Pineapple Slices with Greek Yogurt

- *Difficulty Level:* ☐
- *Preparation Time: 10 minutes*
- *Cooking Time: 5 minutes*
- *Cooking Level: Easy*

Ingredients:

- *4 slices of fresh pineapple*
- *1 cup Greek yogurt*
- *2 tablespoons honey*
- *1 teaspoon vanilla extract*
- *Fresh mint leaves for garnish (optional)*

Instructions:

Preparation:
1. Preheat your grill or grill pan to medium-high heat.

2. In a small bowl, mix the Greek yogurt, honey, and vanilla extract until well combined. This will be used as a dipping sauce for the grilled pineapple.

Grilling:
1. Place the pineapple slices on the grill grates or grill pan. Grill for about 2-3 minutes per side, or until you see grill marks and the pineapple becomes slightly caramelized.

2. Once the pineapple slices are nicely grilled, remove them from the grill and let them cool for a minute.

Serving:
1. Serve the grilled pineapple slices on a plate.

2. Place a dollop of the honey and vanilla Greek yogurt mixture on the side or in the center.

3. If desired, garnish with fresh mint leaves for a pop of color and extra freshness.

4. Serve the grilled pineapple with the Greek yogurt dip as a tasty and healthy dessert.

Enjoy the delightful combination of grilled pineapple and creamy Greek yogurt!

Nutritional Values (per serving):

Calories: 180

Protein: 8g

Fat: 0.5g

Carbohydrates: 40g

Fiber: 2g

Sugar: 34g

Glycemic Index (GI): Grilled pineapple has a moderate GI due to natural sugars. The yogurt and honey mixture can help balance the GI, making it a healthier dessert option.

Strawberry Coconut Chia Smoothie Bowl

- Difficulty Level: ☐
- Preparation Time: 10 minutes
- Cooking Time: 0 minutes
- Cooking Level: Easy

Ingredients:

For the Smoothie Base:

- 1 cup fresh or frozen strawberries
- 1/2 cup coconut milk (or any milk of your choice)
- 1 ripe banana
- 2 tablespoons Greek yogurt
- 1 tablespoon honey (optional)
- 1 tablespoon chia seeds

Toppings:

- Sliced strawberries
- Shredded coconut
- Chia seeds
- Granola
- Fresh mint leaves for garnish (optional)

Instructions:

Preparation:

1. Start by preparing the smoothie base. In a blender, combine the strawberries, coconut milk, ripe banana, Greek yogurt, honey (if using), and chia seeds.

2. Blend until the mixture is smooth and well combined. If the smoothie is too thick, you can add a bit more milk to reach your desired consistency.

Serving:

1. Pour the smoothie into a bowl.

2. Arrange your choice of toppings on the smoothie as desired. You can use sliced strawberries, shredded coconut, chia seeds, granola, and garnish with fresh mint leaves, if you like.

3. Your strawberry coconut chia smoothie bowl is ready to enjoy!

Feel free to get creative with your choice of toppings and create your own beautiful and delicious smoothie bowl. It's a perfect, healthy breakfast or snack option.

Nutritional Values (including suggested toppings, per serving):

Calories: 400

Protein: 7g

Fat: 18g

Carbohydrates: 55g

Fiber: 9g

Sugar: 26g

Glycemic Index (GI): The GI of this smoothie bowl is moderate due to natural sugars from the fruits and honey. The addition of chia seeds, coconut, and granola helps provide a balanced, sustained energy release.

Grilled Peach with Almonds and Honey

- Difficulty Level: □□
- Preparation Time: 10 minutes
- Cooking Time: 5 minutes
- Cooking Level: Easy

Ingredients:

- 2 ripe peaches, halved and pitted
- 2 tablespoons sliced almonds
- 2 tablespoons honey
- 1/2 teaspoon ground cinnamon
- A pinch of salt
- Vanilla ice cream or Greek yogurt (optional)

Instructions:

Preparation:

1. Preheat your grill to medium-high heat.

2. In a small bowl, mix the sliced almonds, honey, ground cinnamon, and a pinch of salt to create the almond and honey glaze.

Grilling:

1. Place the peach halves, cut side down, directly on the grill grates.

2. Grill the peaches for about 2-3 minutes on each side or until you get nice grill marks and the peaches are slightly softened. Be careful not to overcook them; you want them to remain firm enough to handle.

Serving:

1. Remove the grilled peaches from the grill and place them on a serving plate, cut side up.

2. Drizzle the almond and honey glaze over the grilled peaches.

3. If desired, you can serve them with a scoop of vanilla ice cream or a dollop of Greek yogurt.

4. Serve immediately while still warm. The combination of the warm, caramelized peaches with the honey-almond glaze is delightful.

Enjoy your grilled peaches with almonds and honey as a delicious and healthy dessert!

Nutritional Values (per serving, without optional ice cream or yogurt):

Calories: 180

Protein: 3g

Fat: 6g

Carbohydrates: 32g

Fiber: 4g

Sugar: 27g

Glycemic Index (GI): The GI of grilled peaches is relatively low, making them a good choice for a healthy dessert. Honey can increase the GI slightly, but it's balanced by the fiber and nutrients in the peaches.

Crepes with Strawberries and Light Whipped Cream

- Difficulty Level: ☐☐
- Preparation Time: 15 minutes
- Cooking Time: 20 minutes
- Cooking Level: Intermediate

Ingredients:

For the Crepes:

- 1 cup all-purpose flour
- 2 eggs
- 1/2 cup milk
- 1/2 cup water
- 2 tablespoons melted butter
- 1/4 teaspoon salt
- 1 tablespoon granulated sugar
- 1 teaspoon vanilla extract

For the Filling:

- 2 cups fresh strawberries, hulled and sliced
- 1 cup light whipped cream
- Powdered sugar for dusting

Instructions:

Preparation:

1. In a blender, combine the flour, eggs, milk, water, melted butter, salt, granulated sugar, and vanilla extract. Blend until the batter is smooth. Let the batter rest for at least 30 minutes. This will allow any air bubbles to

dissipate, resulting in crepes that are less likely to tear during cooking.

2. While the crepe batter is resting, prepare the strawberries by slicing them.

Cooking the Crepes:

1. Heat a lightly greased non-stick skillet or crepe pan over medium-high heat.

2. Pour 1/4 cup of crepe batter into the center of the skillet and swirl it around to spread the batter thinly over the bottom. You want a thin, even layer.

3. Cook the crepe for about 2 minutes, or until the edges begin to lift and it's easy to slide a spatula under the crepe. Gently flip the crepe and cook for another 1-2 minutes on the other side, or until lightly golden.

4. Transfer the cooked crepe to a plate and repeat the process with the remaining batter. Stack the crepes on the plate, placing a sheet of wax paper or parchment paper between each one to prevent sticking.

Assembling the Crepes:

1. Lay one crepe flat on a serving plate.

2. Place a few slices of fresh strawberries on one-half of the crepe.

3. Fold the other half of the crepe over the strawberries, creating a half-moon shape.

4. Repeat this process with the remaining crepes.

5. Top each crepe with a dollop of light whipped cream.

6. Dust the crepes with powdered sugar for a sweet finish.

7. Serve immediately while the crepes are warm.

These crepes make for a delightful and elegant dessert or breakfast option. Enjoy your crepes with strawberries and light whipped cream!

Nutritional Values (per serving):

Calories: 250
Protein: 5g
Fat: 9g
Carbohydrates: 37g
Fiber: 2g
Sugar: 9g

Glycemic Index (GI): The GI of crepes varies depending on the ingredients used. Traditional crepes made with white flour have a moderate to high GI. Using whole wheat flour would lower the GI. The strawberries in this recipe have a low GI, making this a balanced option.

Greek Yogurt with Kiwi and Flaxseeds

- Difficulty Level: □
- Preparation Time: 5 minutes
- Cooking Time: 0 minutes
- Cooking Level: Easy

Ingredients:

- o 1 cup Greek yogurt
- o 2 ripe kiwis, peeled and sliced
- o 1 tablespoon flaxseeds
- o Honey (optional, for drizzling)

Instructions:

Preparation:

1. Ensure you have ripe kiwis, and peel them. Slice the kiwis into rounds or any desired shape for your presentation.

2. Measure the flaxseeds.

Assembly:

1. Take a serving bowl or glass and add the Greek yogurt.

2. Place the sliced kiwis on top of the yogurt.

3. Sprinkle the flaxseeds over the kiwis.

4. If you desire a touch of sweetness, you can drizzle some honey over the yogurt, kiwi, and flaxseeds.

5. Serve immediately, and enjoy your healthy and delicious Greek yogurt with kiwi and flaxseeds.

Nutritional Values (for the entire serving):

Calories: 300
Protein: 20g
Fat: 6g
Carbohydrates: 45g
Fiber: 9g
Sugar: 25g

Glycemic Index (GI): The glycemic index of this yogurt with kiwi and flaxseeds is low. Kiwis and flaxseeds are low-GI foods, which makes this a great choice for maintaining steady blood sugar levels. If you choose to add honey, the GI will increase slightly due to the natural sugars in honey.

Fruit Salad with Lime and Mint

- Difficulty Level: ☐
- Preparation Time: 15 minutes
- Cooking Time: 0 minutes
- Cooking Level: Easy

Ingredients:

- 2 cups mixed fresh fruits (e.g., strawberries, blueberries, grapes, kiwi, oranges, and melon), washed, peeled, and diced
- 1 lime, zested and juiced
- 2 tablespoons fresh mint leaves, chopped
- 1-2 tablespoons honey (optional, for added sweetness)

Instructions:

Preparation:

1. Wash, peel, and dice the mixed fresh fruits as desired.

2. Zest the lime, then juice it. Set aside the zest and juice.

3. Chop the fresh mint leaves.

Assembly:

1. In a large serving bowl, combine the diced mixed fruits.

2. Drizzle the lime juice over the fruits.

3. Sprinkle the lime zest and chopped fresh mint leaves over the fruits.

4. If you desire a sweeter flavor, you can drizzle honey over the salad.

5. Gently toss the fruit salad to ensure the lime juice, zest, and mint are evenly distributed.

6. Refrigerate for 30 minutes to let the flavors meld, or serve immediately.

7. Enjoy your refreshing and healthy fruit salad with lime and mint.

Nutritional Values (for the entire serving):

Calories: 150

Protein: 2g

Fat: 0.5g

Carbohydrates: 38g

Fiber: 5g

Sugar: 28g

Glycemic Index (GI): The glycemic index of this fruit salad is relatively low since it primarily consists of fresh fruits, which are generally low-GI foods. If you choose to add honey for sweetness, the GI will increase slightly due to the natural sugars in honey.

Banana with Almond Butter and Grated Coconut

- *Difficulty Level:* □
- *Preparation Time: 5 minutes*
- *Cooking Time: 0 minutes*
- *Cooking Level: Easy*

Ingredients:

- *1 ripe banana*
- *1-2 tablespoons almond butter*
- *1-2 tablespoons grated coconut (unsweetened)*

Instructions:

Preparation:

1. Peel the ripe banana and slice it into rounds.

Assembly:

1. Spread almond butter on each banana round.

2. Sprinkle grated coconut over the almond butter.

3. You can garnish with a little extra grated coconut on top for added flavor.

4. Serve and enjoy your simple and delicious banana with almond butter and grated coconut.

Nutritional Values:

The nutritional values for this snack can vary based on the amount of almond butter and coconut you use. On average, it can provide approximately:

Calories: 150

Protein: 2g

Fat: 8g

Carbohydrates: 20g

Fiber: 4g

Sugar: 11g

Glycemic Index (GI): The glycemic index of this snack is low because bananas have a low GI, and almond butter and grated coconut don't significantly affect it. However, be mindful of portion sizes for calorie control.

Banana Fritters with Blueberries

- *Difficulty Level:* □□
- *Preparation Time: 15 minutes*
- *Cooking Time: 15 minutes*
- *Cooking Level: Intermediate*

Ingredients:

- *2 ripe bananas*
- *1 cup all-purpose flour*
- *2 tablespoons sugar*
- *1 teaspoon baking powder*
- *A pinch of salt*
- *1/2 cup milk (you can use regular or a dairy-free alternative)*
- *1 egg*
- *1 teaspoon vanilla extract*
- *1/2 cup blueberries*
- *Cooking oil for frying*

Instructions:

Preparation:

1. In a mixing bowl, mash the ripe bananas until smooth.

2. In a separate bowl, combine the flour, sugar, baking powder, and a pinch of salt.

3. In another bowl, whisk together the milk, egg, and vanilla extract.

Cooking:

1. Pour the wet ingredients (milk mixture) into the dry ingredients (flour mixture) and stir until you have a smooth batter.

2. Gently fold the mashed bananas and blueberries into the batter.

3. In a skillet, heat the cooking oil over medium heat.

4. Using a spoon, carefully drop spoonfuls of the batter into the hot oil. Cook until golden brown, usually 2-3 minutes per side.

5. Remove the fritters from the oil and place them on a paper towel-lined plate to remove excess oil.

6. Serve the banana fritters with blueberries while they're still warm. You can dust them with powdered sugar or drizzle them with honey if desired.

Nutritional Values (per serving):

Calories: 220

Protein: 4g

Fat: 3g

Carbohydrates: 45g

Fiber: 3g

Sugar: 16g

Glycemic Index (GI): The glycemic index of this dish is moderate due to the presence of ripe bananas and sugar. It's a delicious treat but should be consumed in moderation if you're watching your sugar intake.

Pineapple Spinach and Avocado Smoothie

- Difficulty Level: ☐
- Preparation Time: 5 minutes
- Cooking Time: 0 minutes
- Cooking Level: Easy

Ingredients:

- 1 cup fresh pineapple chunks
- 1 cup fresh spinach leaves
- 1/2 ripe avocado
- 1 cup coconut water (or water)
- 1 tablespoon honey (optional for added sweetness)

Instructions:

Preparation:

1. Cut the fresh pineapple into chunks.

2. Wash the fresh spinach leaves and remove any tough stems.

3. Cut the avocado in half, remove the pit, and scoop out the flesh.

Instructions:

1. In a blender, combine the fresh pineapple

chunks, fresh spinach leaves, ripe avocado, and coconut water.

2. If you prefer your smoothie to be a bit sweeter, you can add honey to taste.

3. Blend all the ingredients until you have a smooth and creamy mixture.

4. Pour the smoothie into a glass and serve immediately. Enjoy your refreshing and healthy pineapple spinach and avocado smoothie!

Nutritional Values (per serving):

Calories: 250
Protein: 3g
Fat: 14g
Carbohydrates: 34g
Fiber: 9g
Sugar: 20g

Glycemic Index (GI): This smoothie has a low glycemic index because it's mainly composed of fruits and vegetables, which release sugar into the bloodstream slowly. The addition of honey can slightly increase the GI, so adjust the sweetness to your preference.

Sugar-Free Apple Compote with Cinnamon

- Difficulty Level: □
- Preparation Time: 15 minutes
- Cooking Time: 15 minutes
- Cooking Level: Easy

Ingredients:

- 4 apples, peeled, cored, and chopped

- ½ cup water
- 1 teaspoon ground cinnamon
- ½ teaspoon lemon juice

Instructions:

Preparation:

1. Peel, core, and chop the apples into small pieces.

Cooking:

2. In a saucepan, combine the chopped apples and water.

3. 2. Sprinkle ground cinnamon over the apples and add lemon juice for a hint of freshness.

4. 3. Place the saucepan over medium heat, cover it, and let the apples simmer for about 10-15 minutes, or until they become soft and start to break down.

5. Stir occasionally to prevent sticking or burning. If the mixture seems too dry, you can add a bit more water.

6. Once the apples have reached a compote-like consistency, remove the saucepan from the heat.

7. Allow the compote to cool slightly, and then transfer it to a clean, airtight container.

8. You can serve the sugar-free apple compote warm or chilled, depending on your preference. It's a great topping for

yogurt, oatmeal, pancakes, or as a standalone treat.

Nutritional Values (per serving, approximately ½ cup):

Calories: 50
Protein: 0.3g
Fat: 0.2g
Carbohydrates: 14g
Fiber: 2.5g
Sugar: 10g

Glycemic Index (GI): The glycemic index of this sugar-free apple compote is low, thanks to the absence of added sugars and the fiber content of apples. Cinnamon can also help regulate blood sugar levels.

APPETIZERS

Light Caprese Salad

- Difficulty Level: ☐
- Preparation Time: 10 minutes
- Cooking Time: 0 minutes
- Cooking Skill: Easy

Ingredients:

- Slices of fresh tomato
- Light mozzarella
- Fresh basil leaves
- Extra virgin olive oil
- Salt and pepper (to taste)

Preparation:

1. Cut the slices of fresh tomato into pieces or rounds, depending on your preference. You can also use halved cherry tomatoes for a different twist.

2. Cut the light mozzarella into cubes or thin slices.

3. Arrange the slices of tomato and mozzarella on a serving platter alternately. This will give the salad an appealing look.

4. Distribute the fresh basil leaves among the slices of tomato and mozzarella.

5. Drizzle with extra virgin olive oil. Add salt and pepper to taste.

6. Serve immediately and enjoy Light Caprese Salad as an appetizer or a light side dish.

Nutritional Values (per serving):

Calories: Approximately 150-200 calories
Protein: About 8-10g
Fat: Approximately 10-12g
Carbohydrates: About 5-7g
Fiber: Approximately 2-3g
Sugars: About 3-4g

The glycemic index of Caprese salad is generally low because it contains few carbohydrates and sugars. The GI varies depending on factors such as the ripeness of the tomatoes, the quality of the mozzarella, and the dressing used. However, the GI of Light Caprese Salad tends to be lower compared to many other carbohydrate-based dishes.

Homemade Guacamole with Veggie Sticks:

- *Difficulty Level:* ☐
- *Preparation Time: 15 minutes*
- *Cooking Time: 0 minutes*
- *Cooking Skill: Easy*

Ingredients:

- *3 ripe avocados*
- *1 small red onion, finely diced*
- *2 cloves of garlic, minced*
- *1-2 tomatoes, diced*
- *1 lime, juiced*
- *Salt and pepper to taste*
- *1/2 teaspoon cumin*
- *1/4 teaspoon cayenne pepper (optional for heat)*
- *Fresh cilantro, chopped (optional)*
- *Bell peppers, carrots, and cucumber, cut into sticks, for dipping*

Preparation:

1. *Cut the avocados in half, remove the pits, and scoop the flesh into a bowl.*

2. *Mash the avocados with a fork until you achieve your preferred guacamole consistency (some prefer it chunky, others smooth).*

3. *Add the finely diced red onion, minced garlic, diced tomatoes, lime juice, salt, pepper, cumin, and cayenne pepper (if using).*

4. *Mix all the ingredients thoroughly.*

5. *If you like the flavor of cilantro, add some chopped fresh cilantro to the guacamole.*

6. *Taste and adjust the seasonings as needed.*

7. *Serve the guacamole with the sliced bell peppers, carrots, and cucumber sticks for dipping.*

8. *Enjoy your Homemade Guacamole with Veggie Sticks as a healthy and satisfying snack.*

Nutritional Information (per serving):

Calories: Variable depending on portion size

Protein: Variable

Fat: Variable

Carbohydrates: Variable

Fiber: Variable

Sugars: Variable

Glycemic Index (GI): This snack has a low GI as it primarily consists of healthy fats from avocados and non-starchy vegetables.

Chickpea Hummus with Crudité (for Two): Homemade chickpea hummus served with carrot, bell pepper, celery, and cucumber sticks for two.

- *Difficulty Level:* ☐
- *Preparation Time: 10 minutes*
- *Cooking Time: 0 minutes*
- *Cooking Skill: Easy*

Ingredients:

- 1/2 can (7.5 ounces) of chickpeas, drained and rinsed
- 2 tablespoons tahini (sesame paste)
- 1-2 cloves of garlic, minced
- 1 tablespoon lemon juice
- 1 tablespoon extra-virgin olive oil
- 1/4 teaspoon ground cumin
- Salt and pepper to taste
- Carrot, bell pepper, celery, and cucumber sticks for dipping

Preparation:

1. In a food processor, combine the chickpeas, tahini, minced garlic, lemon juice, extra-virgin olive oil, ground cumin, salt, and pepper.

2. Blend the ingredients until you achieve a smooth and creamy consistency. You may need to scrape down the sides of the bowl and blend again for a consistent texture.

3. Taste the hummus and adjust the seasoning, adding more lemon juice, salt, or cumin if desired.

4. Transfer the hummus to a serving bowl and garnish with a drizzle of olive oil and a pinch of paprika if you like.

5. Arrange the carrot, bell pepper, celery, and cucumber sticks around the hummus for dipping.

6. Serve your Chickpea Hummus with Crudité for two and enjoy this healthy and flavorful appetizer.

Nutritional Values (per serving):

Calories: Approximately 150-200 calories

Protein: About 2-3g

Fat: Approximately 12-15g

Carbohydrates: About 12-15g

Fiber: Approximately 6-8g

Sugars: About 3-4g

The Glycemic Index (GI) of this dish is very low. Since guacamole is primarily made from avocados, which are low in carbohydrates and sugars, and the veggie sticks are also low in carbohydrates, the overall GI is minimal. It's a healthy and nutritious snack option, suitable for those looking to maintain stable blood sugar levels and follow a balanced diet.

Tomato Bruschetta for Two

- *Difficulty Level:* ☐☐
- *Preparation Time: 15 minutes*
- *Cooking Time: 0 minutes*
- *Cooking Skill: Easy*

Ingredients (for Two):

- 2 slices of whole-grain bread
- 1 large ripe tomato, diced
- 1 clove of garlic, minced
- 3-4 fresh basil leaves, chopped
- Extra-virgin olive oil
- Salt and pepper to taste

Preparation:

1. In a bowl, combine the diced tomato, minced garlic, and chopped fresh basil.

2. Drizzle extra-virgin olive oil over the tomato mixture and season with salt and

pepper. Toss everything together to coat the ingredients evenly.

3. Toast the slices of whole-grain bread until they are crisp and golden brown.

4. Spoon the tomato mixture onto the toasted bread slices.

5. Drizzle a little more olive oil on top if desired.

6. Serve your Tomato Bruschetta for Two immediately, and enjoy this classic Italian appetizer.

Nutritional Information (per serving):
Calories: 150-200 kcal
Proteins: 4-6 g
Fats: 6-8 g
Carbohydrates: 20-25 g
Fiber: 3-4 g

The Glycemic Index (GI) of Bruschetta with Tomatoes can vary based on several factors, including the type of bread used and the ripeness of the tomatoes. However, typically, whole-grain bread has a lower GI compared to white bread. Additionally, fresh tomatoes have a relatively low GI.

Salmon Smoked Rolls

- Cooking Time: No cooking required
- Cooking Skill: Easy
- Difficulty Level: ☐
- Preparation Time: 15 minutes

Ingredients:

- 4 slices of smoked salmon

- 4 tablespoons of light cream cheese
- Fresh herbs (such as dill, chives, or parsley)
- Freshly ground black pepper
- Lemon wedges for serving (optional)

Instructions:

1. Lay the smoked salmon slices on a clean work surface.

Preparation:

2. In a small bowl, mix the light cream cheese with freshly chopped herbs of your choice. Common options include dill, chives, or parsley. Add a dash of freshly ground black pepper to taste.

3. Gently spread the herbed cream cheese mixture evenly over each slice of smoked salmon.

Directions:

4. Carefully roll each salmon slice to create a neat roll.

5. If desired, cut each roll into bite-sized pieces for serving.

6. Serve the smoked salmon rolls with lemon wedges on the side if you like a citrusy touch.

Nutritional Information (per serving):

Calories: Approximately 85-100 kcal (varies based on the salmon and cream cheese used)
Protein: 6-8g

Fat: 5-6g

Carbohydrates: 2-3g

Fiber: 0g

Sugar: 0g

Glycemic Index (GI): The salmon rolls are a low-GI food as they do not contain significant carbohydrates. The GI of the salmon itself is negligible, while the cream cheese has a low GI. Enjoy these rolls as a healthy and low-GI appetizer or snack.

Chickpea Salad:

- *Difficulty: ☐☐
- Prep Time: 15 minutes
- Cooking Time: 0 minutes
- Servings: 2

Ingredients:

- 1 can (400g) of cooked chickpeas, drained and rinsed
- 1 ripe tomato, diced
- 1 cucumber, diced
- 1/4 red onion, finely sliced
- 2 tablespoons of fresh parsley, chopped
- 2 tablespoons of extra virgin olive oil
- 1 tablespoon of red wine vinegar
- Salt and freshly ground black pepper, to taste

Instructions:

- In a large bowl, combine the cooked chickpeas, diced tomato, diced cucumber, thinly sliced red onion, and chopped fresh parsley.

- In a small bowl, mix the extra virgin olive oil and red wine vinegar to create the vinaigrette.

- Pour the vinaigrette over the ingredients in the other bowl.

- Mix the chickpea salad well, making sure all the ingredients are evenly coated with the vinaigrette. Adjust the seasoning with salt and pepper to taste.

- Cover the salad and refrigerate it for at least 30 minutes before serving. This will allow the flavors to meld nicely.

- When serving, garnish the chickpea salad with some additional fresh parsley if desired.

Nutritional Information (per serving):

Calories: about 300

Protein: about 10g

Fat: about 14g

Carbohydrates: about 35g

Fiber: about 8g

Sugars: about 6g

Glycemic Index (GI): The Chickpea Salad is considered to have a moderate glycemic index. Chickpeas have a relatively low GI, and the fact that they are combined with fresh vegetables helps keep it stable.

Tzatziki Sauce with Veggie Sticks:

- Difficulty: ☐☐
- Preparation Time: 10 minutes
- Cooking Time: 0 minutes

- *Cooking Skill: Easy*

Servings: 2

Ingredients:

- *1 cup Greek yogurt*
- *1/2 cucumber, grated*
- *1 clove garlic, minced*
- *1 tablespoon fresh mint, chopped*
- *Juice of half a lemon*
- *Carrot and celery sticks for serving*
- *Salt and black pepper to taste*

Instructions:

1. *In a bowl, combine the Greek yogurt, grated cucumber, minced garlic, chopped fresh mint, and lemon juice.*
2. *Mix everything together until the ingredients are well incorporated.*
3. *Season with salt and black pepper to taste.*
4. *Refrigerate the tzatziki sauce for at least 30 minutes before serving to allow the flavors to meld.*
5. *Serve with carrot and celery sticks for dipping.*

Nutritional Information (per serving):

Calories: Approximately 80

Protein: Approximately 5g

Fat: Approximately 2g

Carbohydrates: Approximately 11g

Fiber: Approximately 2g

Sugar: Approximately 5g

Glycemic Index (GI): The glycemic index of tzatziki sauce is low, given its main ingredients (Greek yogurt and vegetables). When served

with carrot and celery sticks, the overall glycemic index of this dish remains low, making it a healthy and balanced choice.

Beet Hummus:

- *Cooking Skill: Easy*
- *Prep Time: 15 minutes*
- *Cook Time: 0 minutes*
- *Servings: 2*

Ingredients:

- *1 can (15 oz) chickpeas, drained and rinsed*
- *2 small roasted beets (about 1 cup), peeled and diced*
- *1/4 cup tahini*
- *2 cloves garlic, minced*
- *3 tablespoons lemon juice*
- *2 tablespoons extra-virgin olive oil, plus extra for drizzling*
- *1/2 teaspoon ground cumin*
- *Salt and pepper, to taste*
- *Fresh parsley, for garnish*

Instructions:

1. *In a food processor, combine the chickpeas, roasted beets, tahini, minced garlic, lemon juice, 2 tablespoons of extra-virgin olive oil, ground cumin, salt, and pepper.*

2. *Process the ingredients until the mixture is smooth and well combined. You may need to scrape down the sides of the food processor a few times to ensure everything is blended evenly.*

3. *Taste the beet hummus and adjust the*

seasoning, adding more salt, pepper, or
lemon juice if desired.

4. Once the beet hummus reaches your
   desired consistency and flavor, transfer
   it to a serving bowl.

5. Drizzle a bit of extra-virgin olive oil
   over the top and garnish with fresh
   parsley.

6. Serve the beet hummus with your
   favorite vegetable sticks, pita bread, or
   as a colorful spread for sandwiches and
   wraps.

Nutritional Information (per serving):

Calories: Approximately 220

Protein: 7g

Fat: 13g

Carbohydrates: 21g

Fiber: 6g

Sugar: 3g

Glycemic Index (GI): The GI of beet hummus is
moderate due to the chickpeas and beets.
Chickpeas have a low to moderate GI, while
beets have a moderate GI. This hummus is a
flavorful and colorful addition to your
appetizer spread.

Gravlax Salmon:

- Cooking Skill: Intermediate
- Prep Time: 10 minutes
- Marinating Time: 2-3 days
- Servings: 2

Ingredients:

- 8 oz (about 225g) fresh salmon fillet,
  skin-on
- 1/4 cup salt
- 1/4 cup granulated sugar
- 1 tablespoon crushed juniper berries
- 1 tablespoon crushed dill seeds
- 1/2 cup fresh dill, chopped
- Freshly ground black pepper
- Rye or whole-grain bread, for serving
- Dijon mustard, for serving

Instructions:

1. In a small bowl, mix together the salt,
   sugar, crushed juniper berries, and
   crushed dill seeds.

2. Lay out a large piece of plastic wrap,
   about twice the length of your salmon
   fillet.

3. Spread half of the salt and sugar
   mixture on the plastic wrap.

4. Lay the salmon fillet, skin-side down, on
   top of the salt mixture.

5. Spread the remaining salt and sugar
   mixture over the salmon.

6. Sprinkle the chopped dill and a
   generous amount of freshly ground
   black pepper evenly over the salmon.

7. Wrap the salmon tightly in the plastic
   wrap and then wrap it in aluminum foil.

8. Place the wrapped salmon in a dish or
   on a baking sheet to catch any potential
   leaks.

9. Refrigerate the salmon for 2-3 days, turning it every 12 hours.

10. When the salmon is ready, unwrap it and scrape off the marinade. Slice it very thinly on a slight diagonal.

11. Serve the gravlax salmon with rye or whole-grain bread and Dijon mustard.

Nutritional Information (per serving):

Calories: Approximately 230

Protein: 22g

Fat: 15g

Carbohydrates: 11g

Fiber: 1g

Sugar: 8g

Glycemic Index (GI): The GI of gravlax salmon is very low since it's essentially raw fish with no carbohydrates. Enjoy this delicacy as an appetizer or part of a meal.

SOUP

Seasonal Vegetable Minestrone (for Two)

- Difficulty Level: ☐☐
- Preparation Time: 15 minutes
- Cooking Time: 30 minutes
- Cooking Skill: Moderate
- Servings: 2

Ingredients:

- 1 zucchini, diced
- 1 carrot, diced
- 1 potato, diced
- 1/2 onion, chopped
- 2 garlic cloves, minced
- 1 celery stalk, sliced
- 1 cup fresh tomatoes, peeled and chopped
- 1/2 cup peas (fresh or frozen)
- 1/2 cup green beans, chopped
- 4 cups vegetable broth
- 1 cup whole-grain pasta (of your choice)
- 1 tablespoon olive oil
- Salt and black pepper, to taste
- Fresh parsley for garnish (optional)

Instructions:

1. In a large pot, heat the olive oil over medium heat. Add the onion and garlic and sauté for a few minutes until they become translucent.

2. Add the zucchini, carrot, potato, and celery. Cook for 5-7 minutes or until the vegetables begin to soften.

3. Pour in the vegetable broth and tomatoes into the pot. Bring to a boil, then reduce the heat and let it simmer covered for about 10 minutes.

4. Add the peas, green beans, and pasta. Cook until the pasta is al dente and the vegetables are tender but still slightly crunchy. Be sure to follow the pasta's cooking time instructions on the package.

5. Taste the minestrone and adjust the seasoning with salt and black pepper to your liking.

6. Serve the hot minestrone, garnishing with fresh parsley if desired.

Nutritional Information (per serving):

Calories: about 300-350

Protein: about 8-10g

Fat: about 5-7g

Carbohydrates: about 60-65g

Fiber: about 12-14g

Sugar: about 10-12g

The Glycemic Index (GI) of the seasonal vegetable minestrone is moderate thanks to the use of whole-grain pasta and vegetables. This recipe is an excellent choice for a healthy and flavorful meal. Enjoy your meal!

Lentil Soup with Tomatoes and Spinach (for Two)

- *Difficulty Level: ▢*
- *Preparation Time: 10 minutes*
- *Cooking Time: 30 minutes*
- *Cooking Skill: Easy*
- *Servings: 2*

Ingredients:

- *1 cup green or brown lentils, rinsed and drained*
- *1/2 onion, chopped*
- *2 cloves garlic, minced*
- *1 carrot, diced*
- *1 celery stalk, sliced*
- *1 can (14 oz) diced tomatoes*
- *4 cups vegetable broth*
- *1/2 teaspoon ground cumin*
- *1/2 teaspoon ground coriander*
- *1/4 teaspoon paprika*
- *Salt and black pepper to taste*
- *2 cups fresh spinach leaves*
- *1 tablespoon olive oil*
- *Fresh lemon juice (optional, for serving)*

- *Fresh parsley for garnish (optional)*

Instructions:

1. *In a large pot, heat the olive oil over medium heat. Add the onion, garlic, carrot, and celery. Sauté for about 5 minutes or until the vegetables become tender.*

2. *Add the lentils, canned tomatoes, vegetable broth, cumin, coriander, paprika, salt, and black pepper to the pot. Stir well.*

3. *Bring the mixture to a boil, then reduce the heat and let it simmer for approximately 25-30 minutes. Make sure the lentils are soft and cooked through.*

4. *Add the fresh spinach leaves and cook for an additional 2-3 minutes until they wilt.*

5. *Taste the lentil soup and adjust the seasoning with salt and pepper as needed.*

6. *Serve the hot soup, garnishing with a squeeze of fresh lemon juice and fresh parsley if you like.*

Nutritional Information (per serving):

Calories: about 300-350

Protein: about 15-18g

Fat: about 5-7g

Carbohydrates: about 50-60g

Fiber: about 15-18g

Sugar: about 6-8g

The Glycemic Index (GI) of the lentil soup is low due to the presence of lentils, which have a low GI. It's a nutritious and filling soup, perfect for a satisfying and healthy meal. Enjoy!

Pumpkin Soup with Cinnamon and Nutmeg (for Two)

- Difficulty Level: ☐
- Preparation Time: 10 minutes
- Cooking Time: 25 minutes
- Cooking Skill: Easy
- Servings: 2

Ingredients:

- 2 cups pumpkin puree (canned or homemade)
- 1/2 onion, chopped
- 2 cloves garlic, minced
- 2 cups vegetable broth
- 1/2 teaspoon ground cinnamon
- 1/4 teaspoon ground nutmeg
- Salt and black pepper to taste
- 1/2 cup coconut milk (or heavy cream for a richer version)
- 1 tablespoon olive oil
- Fresh parsley or chives for garnish (optional)

Instructions:

1. In a pot, heat the olive oil over medium heat. Add the chopped onion and minced garlic. Sauté for about 5 minutes or until the onion becomes translucent.

2. Add the pumpkin puree, vegetable broth, ground cinnamon, ground nutmeg, salt,

and black pepper to the pot. Stir well to combine.

3. Bring the mixture to a boil, then reduce the heat and let it simmer for approximately 20-25 minutes, allowing the flavors to meld.

4. Stir in the coconut milk and continue to cook for an additional 5 minutes. If you prefer a richer soup, you can use heavy cream instead of coconut milk.

5. Taste the pumpkin soup and adjust the seasoning with salt and pepper as needed.

6. Serve the hot soup, garnished with a sprinkle of fresh parsley or chives if you like.

Nutritional Information (per serving):

Calories: about 200-250
Protein: about 3-5g
Fat: about 10-12g
Carbohydrates: about 25-30g
Fiber: about 5-7g
Sugar: about 8-10g

The Glycemic Index (GI) of pumpkin is relatively low, and with the addition of spices and broth, this soup maintains a low to moderate GI. It's a comforting and flavorful choice for a meal. Enjoy!

Pumpkin Soup with Cinnamon and Nutmeg (for Two)

- Difficulty Level: ☐

- *Preparation Time: 10 minutes*
- *Cooking Time: 25 minutes*
- *Cooking Skill: Easy*
- *Servings: 2*

Ingredients:

- *2 cups pumpkin puree (canned or homemade)*
- *1/2 onion, chopped*
- *2 cloves garlic, minced*
- *2 cups vegetable broth*
- *1/2 teaspoon ground cinnamon*
- *1/4 teaspoon ground nutmeg*
- *Salt and black pepper to taste*
- *1/2 cup coconut milk (or heavy cream for a richer version)*
- *1 tablespoon olive oil*
- *Fresh parsley or chives for garnish (optional)*

Instructions:

1. *In a pot, heat the olive oil over medium heat. Add the chopped onion and minced garlic. Sauté for about 5 minutes or until the onion becomes translucent.*

2. *Add the pumpkin puree, vegetable broth, ground cinnamon, ground nutmeg, salt, and black pepper to the pot. Stir well to combine.*

3. *Bring the mixture to a boil, then reduce the heat and let it simmer for approximately 20-25 minutes, allowing the flavors to meld.*

4. *Stir in the coconut milk and continue to cook for an additional 5 minutes. If you prefer a richer soup, you can use heavy cream instead of coconut milk.*

5. *Taste the pumpkin soup and adjust the seasoning with salt and pepper as needed.*

6. *Serve the hot soup, garnished with a sprinkle of fresh parsley or chives if you like.*

Nutritional Information (per serving):

Calories: about 200-250

Protein: about 3-5g

Fat: about 10-12g

Carbohydrates: about 25-30g

Fiber: about 5-7g

Sugar: about 8-10g

The Glycemic Index (GI) of pumpkin is relatively low, and with the addition of spices and broth, this soup maintains a low to moderate GI. It's a comforting and flavorful choice for a meal. Enjoy!

Tomato Soup with Fresh Basil (for Two)

- *Difficulty Level: ☐*
- *Preparation Time: 10 minutes*
- *Cooking Time: 20 minutes*
- *Cooking Skill: Easy*
- *Servings: 2*

Ingredients:

- *2 cups canned tomato puree or crushed tomatoes*
- *1 cup vegetable broth*
- *1/2 cup diced onion*
- *2 cloves garlic, minced*

- *2 tablespoons fresh basil leaves, chopped*
- *1/4 cup heavy cream or coconut milk (for a dairy-free option)*
- *2 tablespoons olive oil*
- *Salt and black pepper to taste*
- *Fresh basil leaves for garnish (optional)*

Instructions:

1. *In a pot, heat the olive oil over medium heat. Add the diced onion and minced garlic. Sauté for about 5 minutes or until the onion is soft and translucent.*

2. *Pour in the canned tomato puree or crushed tomatoes and vegetable broth. Stir well to combine.*

3. *Bring the mixture to a simmer, then reduce the heat and let it cook for approximately 15-20 minutes, allowing the flavors to meld.*

4. *Stir in the fresh basil and heavy cream (or coconut milk for a dairy-free version). Continue to cook for an additional 5 minutes.*

5. *Season the tomato soup with salt and black pepper according to your taste.*

6. *Serve the hot soup, garnished with fresh basil leaves if desired.*

Nutritional Information (per serving):

Calories: approximately 180-220

Protein: about 3-5g

Fat: about 12-15g

Carbohydrates: about 15-18g

Fiber: about 4-6g

Sugar: about 8-10g

The Glycemic Index (GI) of tomato soup is low, making it a good choice for a healthy meal. The addition of fresh basil enhances the flavor and nutritional value of this comforting soup. Enjoy!

Chickpea Soup with Spinach and Turmeric

- *Difficulty Level:* ☐☐
- *Preparation Time: 10 minutes*
- *Cooking Time: 20 minutes*
- *Cooking Skill: Intermediate*
- *Servings: 2*

Ingredients:

- *1 can (15 oz) chickpeas, drained and rinsed*
- *2 cups vegetable broth*
- *1 cup fresh spinach, chopped*
- *1/2 onion, finely chopped*
- *2 cloves garlic, minced*
- *1 teaspoon ground turmeric*
- *1/2 teaspoon ground cumin*
- *1/2 teaspoon paprika*
- *2 tablespoons olive oil*
- *Salt and black pepper to taste*
- *Lemon wedges for serving (optional)*

Instructions:

1. *In a pot, heat the olive oil over medium heat. Add the finely chopped onion and minced garlic. Sauté for about 3-4 minutes until the onion becomes translucent.*

2. *Stir in the ground turmeric, ground*

cumin, and paprika. Cook for an additional 2 minutes to toast the spices.

3. Add the chickpeas and vegetable broth to the pot. Bring the mixture to a boil, then reduce the heat and let it simmer for about 15-20 minutes.

4. About 5 minutes before serving, stir in the fresh chopped spinach and let it wilt into the soup. Season with salt and black pepper to taste.

5. Serve the chickpea soup hot, with a squeeze of fresh lemon juice if desired.

Nutritional Information (per serving):

Calories: approximately 250-300
Protein: about 9-12g
Fat: about 10-12g
Carbohydrates: about 30-35g
Fiber: about 7-9g
Sugar: about 3-5g

The Glycemic Index (GI) of chickpea soup is moderate, thanks to the legumes' presence. The addition of turmeric and cumin brings both flavor and potential health benefits. Enjoy this warm and nutritious soup!

Chicken and Vegetable Soup

- Difficulty Level: ☐
- Preparation Time: 15 minutes
- Cooking Time: 30 minutes
- Cooking Skill: Easy
- Servings: 2

Ingredients:

- 2 boneless, skinless chicken breasts, cut into bite-sized pieces
- 4 cups chicken broth
- 1 cup carrots, sliced
- 1 cup celery, sliced
- 1 cup green beans, cut into 1-inch pieces
- 1 cup onion, chopped
- 2 cloves garlic, minced
- 1 bay leaf
- 1 teaspoon dried thyme
- Salt and black pepper to taste
- 2 tablespoons olive oil
- Fresh parsley for garnish (optional)

Instructions:

1. In a large pot, heat the olive oil over medium heat. Add the chopped onion and minced garlic. Sauté for about 3-4 minutes until the onion becomes translucent.

2. Add the chicken pieces and cook until they are no longer pink, about 5-7 minutes.

3. Pour in the chicken broth and add the carrots, celery, green beans, bay leaf, and dried thyme. Season with salt and black pepper to taste.

4. Bring the soup to a boil, then reduce the heat to low and let it simmer for about 20-25 minutes, or until the vegetables are tender and the chicken is cooked through.

5. Remove the bay leaf before serving.

6. Garnish with fresh parsley, if desired.

Nutritional Information (per serving):

Calories: approximately 250-300

Protein: about 25-30g

Fat: about 5-7g

Carbohydrates: about 20-25g

Fiber: about 5-7g

Sugar: about 8-10g

The Glycemic Index (GI) of chicken and vegetable soup is low, making it a healthy and balanced choice for a meal.

Mushroom Soup with Leeks and Parsley

- *Difficulty Level: □□*
- *Preparation Time: 20 minutes*
- *Cooking Time: 25 minutes*
- *Cooking Skill: Intermediate*
- *Servings: 2*

Ingredients:

- *8 oz (about 225g) white or cremini mushrooms, sliced*
- *1 leek, washed and thinly sliced (use the white and light green parts only)*
- *2 cloves garlic, minced*
- *2 tablespoons unsalted butter*
- *2 cups vegetable broth*
- *1/2 cup heavy cream*
- *2 tablespoons fresh parsley, chopped*
- *Salt and black pepper to taste*
- *2 tablespoons olive oil*
- *Crusty bread for serving (optional)*

Instructions:

1. *In a large pot, heat the olive oil over medium heat. Add the sliced leeks and cook for about 4-5 minutes until they become soft and translucent.*

2. *Add the minced garlic and continue to cook for another minute.*

3. *In a separate pan, melt the butter over medium heat. Add the sliced mushrooms and cook until they are browned and any released liquid has evaporated, about 7-8 minutes. Set aside a few mushroom slices for garnish.*

4. *Transfer the cooked mushrooms to the pot with the leeks and garlic. Stir to combine.*

5. *Pour in the vegetable broth and bring the mixture to a boil. Reduce the heat and let it simmer for about 10-15 minutes.*

6. *Use an immersion blender to puree the soup until smooth. Alternatively, you can transfer the soup to a blender, but be careful when blending hot liquids.*

7. *Return the blended soup to the pot, add the heavy cream, and stir well. Cook for an additional 5 minutes.*

8. *Season the soup with salt and black pepper to taste.*

9. *Ladle the soup into bowls, garnish with a dollop of heavy cream (if desired), a few reserved mushroom slices, and a sprinkle of fresh parsley.*

10. Serve hot with crusty bread on the side, if you like.

Nutritional Information (per serving):

Calories: approximately 300-350
Protein: about 6-8g
Fat: about 25-30g
Carbohydrates: about 15-20g
Fiber: about 2-4g
Sugar: about 6-8g

The Glycemic Index (GI) of mushroom soup is relatively low, making it a wholesome choice for your meal.

Pea Soup with Fresh Mint

- Difficulty Level: □□
- Preparation Time: 15 minutes
- Cooking Time: 25 minutes
- Cooking Skill: Intermediate
- Servings: 2

Ingredients:

- 1 cup dried green peas
- 1 small onion, chopped
- 2 cloves garlic, minced
- 2 cups vegetable broth
- 2 tablespoons fresh mint leaves, chopped
- 2 tablespoons olive oil
- Salt and black pepper to taste
- A few fresh mint leaves for garnish (optional)
- Sour cream or yogurt for drizzling (optional)

Instructions:

1. Rinse the dried green peas and soak them in water for a few hours or overnight to soften.

2. In a large pot, heat the olive oil over medium heat. Add the chopped onion and sauté until it becomes translucent, about 5 minutes.

3. Add the minced garlic and sauté for another minute.

4. Drain the soaked peas and add them to the pot. Stir for a few minutes to combine with the onion and garlic.

5. Pour in the vegetable broth and bring the mixture to a boil. Reduce the heat, cover, and simmer for about 20-25 minutes, or until the peas are tender.

6. Use an immersion blender to puree the soup until it reaches a smooth consistency. You can also transfer the soup to a blender, but be cautious with hot liquids.

7. Stir in the chopped fresh mint leaves, reserving a few for garnish.

8. Season the soup with salt and black pepper to taste.

9. Ladle the pea soup into bowls, garnish with a drizzle of sour cream or yogurt (if desired), and a few fresh mint leaves.

Nutritional Information (per serving):

Calories: approximately 250-300

Protein: about 10-12g

Fat: about 7-9g

Carbohydrates: about 35-40g

Fiber: about 10-12g

Sugar: about 8-10g

The Glycemic Index (GI) of pea soup is relatively low, making it a nutritious choice for your meal.

Black Bean Soup with Avocado

- Difficulty Level: ☐☐
- Preparation Time: 15 minutes
- Cooking Time: 25 minutes
- Cooking Skill: Intermediate
- Servings: 2

Ingredients:

- 1 can (15 oz) black beans, drained and rinsed
- 1 small onion, chopped
- 2 cloves garlic, minced
- 1 small red bell pepper, chopped
- 1 small jalapeño pepper, seeds removed and finely chopped (optional for heat)
- 1 teaspoon ground cumin
- 1 teaspoon chili powder
- 2 cups vegetable broth
- 1 ripe avocado, peeled, pitted, and diced
- Juice of 1 lime
- Salt and black pepper to taste
- Fresh cilantro leaves for garnish
- Sour cream or Greek yogurt for drizzling (optional)

Instructions:

1. In a large pot, heat a bit of oil over medium heat. Add the chopped onion and sauté for about 5 minutes or until it becomes translucent.

2. Add the minced garlic, red bell pepper, and jalapeño (if using) to the pot. Sauté for an additional 2-3 minutes until the peppers start to soften.

3. Stir in the cumin and chili powder and cook for another minute, allowing the spices to become fragrant.

4. Add the drained and rinsed black beans to the pot and pour in the vegetable broth.

5. Bring the mixture to a boil, then reduce the heat, cover, and simmer for about 15-20 minutes to allow the flavors to meld.

6. Use an immersion blender to partially puree the soup to your desired consistency. You can leave some chunks for texture.

7. Squeeze in the lime juice, and season with salt and black pepper.

8. Serve the black bean soup in bowls, topped with diced avocado and fresh cilantro. You can also drizzle some sour cream or Greek yogurt if you like.

Nutritional Information (per serving):

Calories: approximately 250-300

Protein: about 8-10g

Fat: about 10-12g

Carbohydrates: about 30-35g

Fiber: about 10-12g
Sugar: about 3-5g

The Glycemic Index (GI) of black bean soup is low, making it a nutritious choice for your meal.

Sweet Potato Soup with Ginger

- Difficulty Level: ☐☐
- Preparation Time: 15 minutes
- Cooking Time: 25 minutes
- Cooking Skill: Intermediate
- Servings: 2

Ingredients:

- 2 medium-sized sweet potatoes, peeled and diced
- 1 small onion, chopped
- 2 cloves garlic, minced
- inch piece of fresh ginger, grated
- 3 cups vegetable broth
- 1/2 cup coconut milk (from a can)
- 1 teaspoon ground cumin
- 1/2 teaspoon ground coriander
- 1/4 teaspoon red pepper flakes (adjust to taste)
- Salt and black pepper to taste
- Fresh cilantro leaves for garnish
- Lime wedges for serving

Instructions:

1- In a large pot, heat a bit of oil over medium heat. Add the chopped onion and sauté for about 5 minutes or until it becomes translucent.

2- Add the minced garlic, grated ginger, cumin, coriander, and red pepper flakes

to the pot. Sauté for an additional 2-3 minutes until fragrant.

3- Add the diced sweet potatoes to the pot and pour in the vegetable broth.

4- Bring the mixture to a boil, then reduce the heat, cover, and simmer for about 15-20 minutes or until the sweet potatoes are tender.

5- Using an immersion blender, puree the soup until smooth.

6- Stir in the coconut milk and continue to simmer for an additional 5 minutes.

7- Season with salt and black pepper to taste.

8- Serve the sweet potato soup in bowls, garnished with fresh cilantro leaves and lime wedges on the side.

Nutritional Information (per serving):

Calories: approximately 250-300
Protein: about 3-5g
Fat: about 10-12g
Carbohydrates: about 35-40g
Fiber: about 6-8g
Sugar: about 10-12g

The Glycemic Index (GI) of sweet potato soup is moderate, and it provides a good source of complex carbohydrates and fiber.

PASTA

Whole Wheat Spaghetti with Basil Pesto and Sun-Dried Tomatoes

- *Difficulty Level:* ☐☐
- *Preparation Time: 15 minutes*
- *Cooking Time: 10 minutes*
- *Cooking Skill: Intermediate*
- *Servings: 2*

Ingredients:

- *200g whole wheat spaghetti*
- *2 cups fresh basil leaves*
- *2 cloves garlic*
- *1/4 cup pine nuts*
- *1/2 cup grated Parmesan cheese*
- *1/2 cup extra-virgin olive oil*
- *1/4 cup sun-dried tomatoes, chopped*
- *Salt and black pepper to taste*
- *Grated Parmesan cheese and fresh basil leaves for garnish*

Instructions:

1- *Cook the whole wheat spaghetti according to the package instructions until al dente. Drain and set aside.*

2- *In a food processor, combine the fresh basil, garlic, pine nuts, and grated Parmesan cheese. Pulse until well blended.*

3- *With the food processor running, slowly drizzle in the extra-virgin olive oil until you have a smooth pesto sauce.*

4- *Season the pesto with salt and black pepper to taste. Adjust the seasoning as needed.*

5- *In a large bowl, toss the cooked whole wheat spaghetti with the basil pesto and chopped sun-dried tomatoes until well coated.*

6- *Divide the pasta between two plates and garnish with additional grated Parmesan cheese and fresh basil leaves.*

Nutritional Information (per serving):

Calories: approximately 600-700
Protein: about 15-20g
Fat: about 45-55g
Carbohydrates: about 45-50g
Fiber: about 10-12g
Sugar: about 4-6g

The Glycemic Index (GI) of whole wheat spaghetti is moderate, and when paired with basil pesto and sun-dried tomatoes, it remains in the moderate range. Enjoy your delicious whole wheat spaghetti with basil pesto and sun-dried tomatoes!

Whole Wheat Penne with Cherry Tomatoes and Eggplant

- *Difficulty Level:* ☐☐
- *Preparation Time: 20 minutes*
- *Cooking Time: 25 minutes*
- *Cooking Skill: Intermediate*
- *Servings: 2*

Ingredients:

- *200g whole wheat penne*
- *1 small eggplant, diced*
- *2 cups cherry tomatoes, halved*
- *2 cloves garlic, minced*
- *1/4 cup fresh basil leaves, chopped*

- 1/4 cup extra-virgin olive oil
- Salt and black pepper to taste
- Grated Parmesan cheese for garnish (optional)

Instructions:

1- Cook the whole wheat penne according to the package instructions until al dente. Drain and set aside.

2- In a large skillet, heat the extra-virgin olive oil over medium heat. Add the diced eggplant and sauté until it becomes tender and slightly golden, about 10-12 minutes.

3- Add the minced garlic and sauté for an additional 1-2 minutes until fragrant.

4- Stir in the halved cherry tomatoes and continue to cook for about 5-7 minutes until they start to soften and release their juices.

5- Season the mixture with salt and black pepper to taste and add the chopped fresh basil. Stir to combine.

6- Add the cooked whole wheat penne to the skillet and toss everything together until the pasta is well coated with the tomato, eggplant, and basil mixture.

7- Serve the whole wheat penne with cherry tomatoes and eggplant hot, garnished with grated Parmesan cheese if desired.

Nutritional Information (per serving):

Calories: approximately 450-500

Protein: about 10-12g

Fat: about 18-20g

Carbohydrates: about 65-70g

Fiber: about 10-12g

Sugar: about 5-6g

The Glycemic Index (GI) of whole wheat penne is moderate, and this dish remains in the moderate range due to the addition of eggplant, tomatoes, and whole wheat pasta. Enjoy your delicious whole wheat penne with cherry tomatoes and eggplant!

Lemon Linguine with Zucchini and Peas

- Difficulty Level: ☐☐
- Preparation Time: 15 minutes
- Cooking Time: 20 minutes
- Cooking Skill: Intermediate
- Servings: 2

Ingredients:

- 200g linguine pasta
- 1 medium zucchini, thinly sliced
- 1/2 cup fresh or frozen peas
- Zest of 1 lemon
- Juice of 1 lemon
- 2 cloves garlic, minced
- 2 tablespoons extra-virgin olive oil
- 1/4 cup fresh basil leaves, chopped
- Salt and black pepper to taste
- Grated Parmesan cheese for garnish (optional)

Instructions:

1- Cook the linguine pasta according to the package instructions until al dente. Drain and set aside.

2- In a large skillet, heat the extra-virgin olive oil over medium heat. Add the sliced zucchini and sauté for about 5 minutes until they start to turn golden.

3- Add the minced garlic and sauté for another 1-2 minutes until fragrant.

4- Stir in the fresh or frozen peas and cook for an additional 5-7 minutes, or until they are heated through and tender.

5- Add the lemon zest and lemon juice to the skillet, then season the mixture with salt and black pepper to taste. Mix well.

6- Add the cooked linguine to the skillet and toss everything together, making sure the pasta is well coated with the lemon, zucchini, and pea mixture.

7- Sprinkle the chopped fresh basil over the linguine and toss gently to combine.

8- Serve the lemon linguine with zucchini and peas hot, garnished with grated Parmesan cheese if desired.

Nutritional Information (per serving):

Calories: approximately 400-450
Protein: about 10-12g
Fat: about 10-12g
Carbohydrates: about 70-75g
Fiber: about 7-8g
Sugar: about 5-6g

The Glycemic Index (GI) of whole wheat linguine is moderate, and this dish remains in the moderate range due to the addition of

zucchini and peas. Enjoy your delicious lemon linguine with zucchini and peas!

Lemon Linguine with Zucchini and Peas

- Difficulty Level: ☐☐
- Preparation Time: 15 minutes
- Cooking Time: 20 minutes
- Cooking Skill: Intermediate
- Servings: 2

Ingredients:

- 200g linguine pasta
- 1 medium zucchini, thinly sliced
- 1/2 cup fresh or frozen peas
- Zest of 1 lemon
- Juice of 1 lemon
- 2 cloves garlic, minced
- 2 tablespoons extra-virgin olive oil
- 1/4 cup fresh basil leaves, chopped
- Salt and black pepper to taste
- Grated Parmesan cheese for garnish (optional)

Instructions:

1- Cook the linguine pasta according to the package instructions until al dente. Drain and set aside.

2- In a large skillet, heat the extra-virgin olive oil over medium heat. Add the sliced zucchini and sauté for about 5 minutes until they start to turn golden.

3- Add the minced garlic and sauté for another 1-2 minutes until fragrant.

4- Stir in the fresh or frozen peas and cook

for an additional 5-7 minutes, or until they are heated through and tender.

5- Add the lemon zest and lemon juice to the skillet, then season the mixture with salt and black pepper to taste. Mix well.

6- Add the cooked linguine to the skillet and toss everything together, making sure the pasta is well coated with the lemon, zucchini, and pea mixture.

7- Sprinkle the chopped fresh basil over the linguine and toss gently to combine.

8- Serve the lemon linguine with zucchini and peas hot, garnished with grated Parmesan cheese if desired.

Nutritional Information (per serving):

Calories: approximately 400-450

Protein: about 10-12g

Fat: about 10-12g

Carbohydrates: about 70-75g

Fiber: about 7-8g

Sugar: about 5-6g

The Glycemic Index (GI) of whole wheat linguine is moderate, and this dish remains in the moderate range due to the addition of zucchini and peas. Enjoy your delicious lemon linguine with zucchini and peas!

Whole Wheat Lasagna with Spinach and Low-Fat Ricotta

- Difficulty Level: ☐☐☐
- Preparation Time: 20 minutes
- Cooking Time: 45 minutes

- Baking Skill: Intermediate
- Servings: 2

Ingredients:

- 6 whole wheat lasagna noodles
- 1 cup low-fat ricotta cheese
- 2 cups fresh spinach leaves
- 1/2 cup grated Parmesan cheese
- 1/2 cup part-skim mozzarella cheese, shredded
- 1/2 cup tomato sauce
- 2 cloves garlic, minced
- 1/2 teaspoon dried basil
- 1/2 teaspoon dried oregano
- Salt and black pepper to taste
- Olive oil for greasing the baking dish

Instructions:

1- Preheat your oven to 375°F (190°C).

2- In a large pot, bring water to a boil and cook the whole wheat lasagna noodles according to the package instructions until al dente. Drain and set aside.

3- In a skillet, heat a small amount of olive oil over medium heat. Add the minced garlic and cook for about 1-2 minutes until fragrant.

4- Add the fresh spinach leaves to the skillet and sauté for 2-3 minutes until they wilt. Remove from heat.

5- In a mixing bowl, combine the low-fat ricotta cheese, grated Parmesan cheese, dried basil, dried oregano, salt, and black pepper.

6- Grease a small baking dish with olive oil. Place 2 cooked lasagna noodles on the bottom.

7- Spread half of the ricotta mixture over the noodles, then layer with half of the wilted spinach. Repeat the process with the remaining noodles, ricotta mixture, and spinach.

8- Top the lasagna with a layer of tomato sauce and sprinkle the shredded mozzarella cheese over it.

9- Cover the baking dish with aluminum foil and bake in the preheated oven for 25 minutes.

10- Remove the foil and bake for an additional 15-20 minutes, or until the lasagna is hot and bubbly, and the cheese is golden and melted.

Nutritional Information (per serving):

Calories: approximately 400-450

Protein: about 30-35g

Fat: about 15-20g

Carbohydrates: about 30-35g

Fiber: about 6-8g

Sugar: about 5-7g

The Glycemic Index (GI) of whole wheat lasagna noodles is moderate, making this lasagna a balanced and nutritious meal. Enjoy your whole wheat lasagna with spinach and low-fat ricotta!

Potato Gnocchi with Arugula Pesto:

- Difficulty Level: ☐ ☐

- Preparation Time: 1 hour
- Cooking Time: 3-5 minutes
- Cooking Skill: Moderate

Ingredients for Potato Gnocchi:

For the Gnocchi Dough:

- 2 large potatoes
- 1 egg
- 1/2 teaspoon salt
- 1 1/2 cups all-purpose flour, plus extra for dusting

For Arugula Pesto:

- 2 cups fresh arugula leaves
- 1/2 cup grated Parmesan cheese
- 1/4 cup pine nuts
- 2 cloves garlic
- 1/4 cup extra-virgin olive oil
- Salt and black pepper to taste

Instructions:

1- Prepare the Potato Gnocchi:

2- Boil the potatoes with their skins on until they're tender. Drain, peel, and mash the potatoes while they're still warm.
3- In a large mixing bowl, combine the mashed potatoes, egg, and salt.
4- Gradually add the flour and knead the mixture until you have a soft dough. Add more flour if needed to prevent sticking.
5- On a floured surface, roll the dough into ropes and cut it into small gnocchi-sized pieces.

Make the Arugula Pesto:

1- In a food processor, combine arugula, Parmesan cheese, pine nuts, and garlic. Pulse until finely chopped.
2- With the processor running, slowly drizzle in the olive oil until you have a smooth pesto. Add salt and black pepper to taste.

Cook the Potato Gnocchi:

1- Bring a large pot of salted water to a boil. Cook the gnocchi in batches for 3-5 minutes, or until they float to the surface. Remove with a slotted spoon and drain.

2- Serve the Gnocchi with Arugula Pesto:

3- Toss the cooked gnocchi with the prepared arugula pesto.
4- Garnish with additional grated Parmesan cheese, pine nuts, and fresh arugula leaves.

Nutritional Information (per serving):

The nutritional values for the gnocchi will depend on the exact size and serving. Here's an approximate estimate for a medium serving:

Calories: about 350-400

Protein: about 10-12g

Fat: about 15-18g

Carbohydrates: about 40-45g

Fiber: about 4-6g

Sugars: about 2-3g

Homemade Pumpkin Ravioli with Butter and Sage

- Difficulty Level: ☐☐☐☐
- Preparation Time: 2 hours
- Cooking Time: 5-7 minutes
- Cooking Skill: Moderate

Ingredients for Homemade Pumpkin Ravioli:

For the Ravioli Dough:

- 2 cups semolina flour
- 3 eggs
- A pinch of salt

For the Pumpkin Filling:

- 1 cup cooked and mashed pumpkin
- 1/2 cup ricotta cheese
- 1/4 cup grated Parmesan cheese
- A pinch of nutmeg
- Salt and black pepper to taste

For the Butter and Sage Sauce:

- 4 tablespoons unsalted butter
- Fresh sage leaves
- Salt and black pepper to taste

Instructions:

Prepare the Ravioli Dough:

1- On a clean surface, create a well with the semolina flour. Crack the eggs into the well and add a pinch of salt.
2- Using a fork, gently whisk the eggs while gradually incorporating the flour.
3- Continue kneading the dough with your hands until it forms a ball. Cover it with plastic wrap and let it rest for at least 30 minutes.

Prepare the Pumpkin Filling:

4- *In a bowl, mix the cooked and mashed pumpkin, ricotta cheese, grated Parmesan cheese, nutmeg, salt, and black pepper. The mixture should be homogeneous. Set it aside.*

Roll Out the Dough:

5- *Divide the dough into two parts. Using a rolling pin or pasta machine, roll each part into thin sheets, aiming to have two equal-sized sheets.*

Fill the Ravioli:

6- *Lay one sheet of pasta on a lightly floured surface. Place small amounts of the pumpkin filling evenly spaced on the sheet.*
7- *Cover with the other sheet of pasta. Press gently around the mounds of filling to seal, then cut the ravioli into shape using a wheel cutter or a ravioli stamp.*

Cook the Ravioli:

8- *Bring a pot of slightly salted water to a boil. Cook the ravioli in boiling water for about 5-7 minutes, or until they float to the surface. Remove them gently.*

Prepare the Butter and Sage Sauce:

9- *In a skillet, melt the butter over medium heat. Add fresh sage leaves and cook until they become crispy.*

10- *Serve the Pumpkin Ravioli:*

11- *Using a slotted spoon, transfer the cooked ravioli to the skillet with butter and sage. Gently toss them to coat with the fragrant sauce.*

Nutritional Information (per serving):

The nutritional values for the ravioli will vary depending on the exact size and filling. Here's an approximate estimate for a medium serving:

Calories: about 350-400

Protein: about 10-12g

Fat: about 15-18g

Carbohydrates: about 40-45g

Fiber: about 4-6g

Sugars: about 2-3g

The Glycemic Index (GI) of Carrot Tagliatelle with Tomato Sauce can be considered low to moderate. The carrots have a lower GI compared to regular pasta, and the tomato sauce helps balance the overall GI of the dish. However, the specific GI value may vary depending on factors like the size of the carrot ribbons and the exact ingredients used. Generally, this dish is a healthier option for those looking to manage blood sugar levels.

Zucchini Noodles with Avocado Pesto

- *Difficulty:* ☐☐
- *Preparation Time: 15 minutes*
- *Cooking Time: 0 minutes*
- *Servings: 2*

Ingredients:

- *2 medium zucchinis*
- *For the Avocado Pesto:*
- *1 ripe avocado*
- *1 garlic clove, minced*

- 1/4 cup fresh basil leaves
- 2 tablespoons lemon juice
- 2 tablespoons toasted walnuts or pine nuts
- 2 tablespoons extra-virgin olive oil
- Salt and freshly ground black pepper, to taste

Instructions:

1- To prepare the avocado pesto, place the ripe avocado, minced garlic, fresh basil, lemon juice, toasted walnuts or pine nuts, extra-virgin olive oil, salt, and black pepper in a high-powered blender or food processor.

2- Blend everything until you have a creamy and smooth mixture. Adjust the seasoning with salt and pepper to your liking. If the pesto is too thick, you can add a little water to reach the desired consistency.

3- Use a spiralizer or a zucchini grater to turn the zucchinis into zucchini noodles.

4- In a large bowl, combine the zucchini noodles with the avocado pesto. Mix well to ensure the zucchinis are evenly coated with the sauce.

5- When serving, you can garnish with fresh basil leaves or some extra toasted walnuts or pine nuts.

Nutritional Information (per serving):

Calories: approximately 350

Protein: approximately 6g

Fat: approximately 30g

Carbohydrates: approximately 18g

Fiber: approximately 8g

Sugars: approximately 4g

These "Zucchini Noodles with Avocado Pesto" are a delicious gluten-free and veggie-packed option. The avocado pesto adds creaminess and flavor to the dish, making it perfect for those looking for a light yet tasty meal. Enjoy!

Carrot Tagliatelle with Tomato Sauce

- *Difficulty Level:* □ □
- *Preparation Time: 20 minutes*
- *Cooking Time: 15 minutes*
- *Cooking Skill: Easy*

Ingredients:

- 2 large carrots
- 1 tablespoon olive oil
- 1 small onion, finely chopped
- 2 cloves garlic, minced
- 1 can (14 oz) crushed tomatoes
- 1 teaspoon dried basil
- 1 teaspoon dried oregano
- Salt and pepper to taste
- Grated Parmesan cheese for garnish (optional)
- Fresh basil leaves for garnish (optional)

Instructions:

1- Peel the carrots and trim the ends. Use a vegetable peeler or a spiralizer to create carrot tagliatelle or ribbons. Set them aside.

2- In a large skillet, heat the olive oil over medium heat. Add the chopped onion and garlic, and sauté until they become soft and fragrant.

3- Pour the crushed tomatoes into the skillet and add the dried basil, dried oregano, salt, and pepper. Stir well to combine. Allow the sauce to simmer for about 10-12 minutes, stirring occasionally.

4- In a separate pot, bring water to a boil. Cook the carrot tagliatelle for about 2-3 minutes or until they become tender but still slightly crisp. Drain them.

5- Serve the carrot tagliatelle with the tomato sauce. Garnish with grated Parmesan cheese and fresh basil leaves if desired.

Nutritional Information (per serving):

Calories: About 120

Protein: About 3g

Fat: About 4g

Carbohydrates: About 20g

Fiber: About 6g

Sugars: About 9g

RISOTTO

Whole Grain Porcini Mushroom Risotto

- Difficulty Level: □ □ □
- Preparation Time: 10 minutes
- Cooking Time: 30 minutes
- Cooking Skill: Medium

Ingredients:

- 1 cup whole grain (brown) rice
- 2 cups vegetable or mushroom broth
- 1 cup dried porcini mushrooms
- 1/2 cup white wine (optional)
- 1/2 cup finely chopped onion
- 2 cloves garlic, minced
- 2 tablespoons olive oil
- 2 tablespoons grated Parmesan cheese
- Salt and black pepper to taste
- Chopped fresh parsley for garnish

Instructions:

- Start by rehydrating the dried porcini mushrooms. Place them in a bowl and cover with hot water. Let them soak for about 20 minutes or until they become soft. Drain the mushrooms and reserve the soaking liquid.

- In a large saucepan, heat the olive oil over medium heat. Add the chopped onion and minced garlic. Sauté until the onion becomes translucent.

- Add the whole grain rice to the pan and stir well to coat it with the oil. Let it toast for a couple of minutes, stirring occasionally.

- If using, pour in the white wine and allow it to cook until mostly evaporated.

- Start adding the mushroom soaking liquid and vegetable or mushroom broth to the rice one ladle at a time. Allow the liquid to be absorbed before adding more. Keep stirring frequently.

- When the rice is almost tender and has a creamy consistency (usually around 25-30 minutes), stir in the rehydrated porcini mushrooms and cook for a few more minutes.

- Remove the risotto from the heat, and stir in the grated Parmesan cheese. Season with salt and black pepper to taste.

- Serve the whole grain porcini mushroom risotto hot, garnished with freshly chopped parsley.

Nutritional Information (per serving):

Calories: approximately 300-350

Protein: 7-8g

Fat: 8-10g

Carbohydrates: 50-55g

Fiber: 5-6g

Sugar: 3-4g

The Glycemic Index (GI) of Whole Grain Porcini Mushroom Risotto can vary based on factors like the specific type and brand of whole grain rice used. Generally, whole grains tend to have a lower GI compared to refined grains. Including mushrooms and vegetables in the risotto can also help in moderating its overall GI.

Whole Grain Lemon Risotto with Green Asparagus (for Two)

- *Difficulty Level:* ☐ ☐ ☐
- *Preparation Time: 10 minutes*
- *Cooking Time: 30 minutes*
- *Cooking Skill: Intermediate*

Ingredients:

For the Risotto:

- *1 cup whole grain Arborio rice*
- *2 tablespoons olive oil*
- *1 small onion, finely chopped*
- *2 cloves garlic, minced*
- *1/2 cup dry white wine*
- *3 cups vegetable broth (approximately)*
- *Zest and juice of 1 lemon*
- *1 bunch of green asparagus, trimmed and cut into 2-inch pieces*
- *Salt and pepper to taste*
- *1/4 cup grated Parmesan cheese (optional for garnish)*
- *Fresh basil leaves for garnish*

Instructions:

1- *In a large skillet or saucepan, heat the olive oil over medium heat. Add the chopped onion and garlic, and sauté until they become translucent, about 2-3 minutes.*

2- *Stir in the Arborio rice and cook for an additional 2-3 minutes, ensuring the rice is well coated with the oil and becomes slightly translucent around the edges.*

3- *Pour in the white wine and cook until it's mostly absorbed by the rice, stirring frequently.*

4- *Begin adding the vegetable broth, one ladle at a time, allowing the liquid to be absorbed by the rice before adding more. Continue this process for about 20-25 minutes until the rice is creamy yet still al dente.*

5- *While the risotto is cooking, blanch the asparagus pieces in boiling water for about 2 minutes, then transfer them to an ice bath to stop the cooking process. Drain and set aside.*

6- *Stir in the lemon zest and juice into the risotto and add the blanched asparagus pieces during the last 3-4 minutes of cooking.*

7- *Season with salt and pepper to taste. If desired, stir in grated Parmesan cheese.*

8- *Remove from heat, cover, and let it rest for a few minutes.*

9- *Serve the lemon risotto garnished with fresh basil leaves and additional Parmesan cheese, if desired.*

Nutritional Information (per serving):

Calories: 350-400

Protein: 7-9g

Fat: 8-10g

Carbohydrates: 60-70g

Fiber: 5-7g

Sugars: 3-4g

Glycemic Index (GI): Whole grain risotto typically has a moderate GI, but the addition of lemon and asparagus may help moderate it further.

Pumpkin Risotto with Rosemary

- *Difficulty Level:* ☐☐
- *Preparation Time: 10 minutes*
- *Cooking Time: 30 minutes*
- *Cooking Skill: Intermediate*

Ingredients:

For the Risotto:

- *1 cup Arborio rice*
- *2 tablespoons olive oil*
- *1 small onion, finely chopped*
- *2 cloves garlic, minced*
- *2 cups diced pumpkin (butternut or any variety)*
- *4 cups vegetable broth (approximately)*
- *2 sprigs of fresh rosemary, leaves removed and finely chopped*
- *1/2 cup dry white wine*
- *Salt and pepper to taste*
- *Grated Parmesan cheese for garnish (optional)*

Instructions:

1- *In a large skillet or saucepan, heat the olive oil over medium heat. Add the chopped onion and garlic, and sauté until they become translucent, about 2-3 minutes.*

2- *Stir in the Arborio rice and cook for an additional 2-3 minutes, ensuring the rice is well coated with the oil and becomes slightly translucent around the edges.*

3- *Add the diced pumpkin and continue to cook for another 2-3 minutes.*

4- *Pour in the white wine and cook until it's mostly absorbed by the rice, stirring frequently.*

5- *Begin adding the vegetable broth, one ladle at a time, allowing the liquid to be absorbed by the rice before adding more. Continue this process for about 20-25 minutes until the rice is creamy* yet still al dente. Stir in the chopped rosemary during the last few minutes of cooking.

6- Season with salt and pepper to taste.

7- Remove from heat, cover, and let it rest for a few minutes.

8- Serve the pumpkin risotto garnished with grated Parmesan cheese, if desired.

Nutritional Information (per serving):

Calories: 350-400

Protein: 6-8g

Fat: 7-9g

Carbohydrates: 70-80g

Fiber: 4-6g

Sugars: 3-4g

Glycemic Index (GI): Whole grain risotto typically has a moderate GI, and the pumpkin might help moderate it further.

Curry Risotto with Peas and Coconut

- Difficulty Level: ☐☐
- Preparation Time: 10 minutes
- Cooking Time: 30 minutes
- Cooking Skill: Intermediate

Ingredients:

- 1 cup Arborio rice
- 2 tablespoons olive oil
- 1 small onion, finely chopped
- 2 cloves garlic, minced
- 1 tablespoon curry powder
- 2 cups vegetable broth (approximately)

- 1/2 cup canned coconut milk
- 1 cup frozen peas
- Salt and pepper to taste
- Fresh cilantro for garnish (optional)
- Lime wedges for serving (optional)

Instructions:

1- In a large skillet or saucepan, heat the olive oil over medium heat. Add the chopped onion and garlic, and sauté until they become translucent, about 2-3 minutes.

2- Stir in the Arborio rice and curry powder. Cook for an additional 2-3 minutes, ensuring the rice is well coated with the oil and curry powder.

3- Begin adding the vegetable broth, one ladle at a time, allowing the liquid to be absorbed by the rice before adding more. Stir frequently.

4- After about 15-20 minutes, stir in the canned coconut milk.

5- Continue adding the vegetable broth and coconut milk in alternating steps until the rice is creamy yet still al dente.

6- Stir in the frozen peas and cook for an additional 2-3 minutes or until they are heated through.

7- Season with salt and pepper to taste.

8- Remove from heat and let it rest for a few minutes.

9- Serve the curry risotto garnished with

fresh cilantro and lime wedges, if
desired.

Nutritional Information (per serving):

Calories: 350-400

Protein: 6-8g

Fat: 7-9g

Carbohydrates: 70-80g

Fiber: 4-6g

Sugars: 3-4g

Glycemic Index (GI): Whole grain rice in
risotto typically has a moderate GI, and the
addition of peas may help moderate it further.
The specific GI can vary depending on the
ingredients and cooking method used.

Red Radicchio and Walnut Risotto (For Two)

- Difficulty Level: ☐☐
- Preparation Time: 10 minutes
- Cooking Time: 25 minutes
- Cooking Skill: Intermediate

Ingredients:

- 1/2 cup Arborio rice
- 1 tablespoon olive oil
- 1/2 small red onion, finely chopped
- 1/2 small head of red radicchio, thinly
  sliced
- 1/4 cup dry white wine
- 2 cups vegetable broth (approximately)
- 1/4 cup chopped walnuts
- 2 tablespoons grated Parmesan cheese
- Salt and pepper to taste

Instructions:

1- In a small saucepan, heat the vegetable
broth over low heat, keeping it warm
but not boiling.

2- In another medium skillet, heat the olive
oil over medium heat. Add the chopped
red onion and cook until it becomes
translucent, about 2-3 minutes.

3- Stir in the Arborio rice and cook for
another 1-2 minutes, making sure the
rice is well coated with the oil.

4- Pour in the white wine and stir until it is
mostly absorbed by the rice.

5- Begin adding the warm vegetable broth,
one ladle at a time, allowing it to be
absorbed by the rice before adding
more. Stir frequently.

6- After about 12-15 minutes, when the
rice is almost done, stir in the sliced
radicchio and continue cooking until it
becomes tender, about 3-5 minutes.

7- Stir in the chopped walnuts and cook for
an additional 2-3 minutes.

8- Remove the skillet from heat and stir in
the grated Parmesan cheese. Season
with salt and pepper to taste.

9- Let the risotto rest for a few minutes
before serving.

Nutritional Information (per serving):

Calories: 400-450

Protein: 10-12g

Fat: 16-18g

Carbohydrates: 50-55g

Fiber: 6-8g

Sugars: 2-3g

Glycemic Index (GI): Risotto made with Arborio rice typically has a moderate GI. The specific GI can vary depending on the ingredients and cooking method used. For a more precise GI value, consult a GI database or a healthcare professional.

CEREALS

Quinoa with Grilled Vegetables and Feta

- Difficulty Level: ☐☐
- Preparation Time: 15 minutes
- Cooking Time: 20 minutes
- Cooking Skill: Intermediate

Ingredients:

- 1 cup quinoa
- 2 cups water or vegetable broth
- 1 red bell pepper, sliced into strips
- 1 zucchini, sliced into rounds
- 1 red onion, sliced into rings
- 1 cup cherry tomatoes
- 1/2 cup crumbled feta cheese
- 2 tablespoons olive oil
- 1/4 cup fresh basil leaves
- Salt and pepper to taste
- Balsamic glaze (optional, for drizzling)

Instructions:

1- Rinse the quinoa thoroughly in a fine mesh strainer. In a medium saucepan, combine the quinoa and water (or vegetable broth). Bring to a boil, then reduce the heat to low, cover, and simmer for about 15 minutes, or until the quinoa is cooked and the liquid is absorbed.

2- While the quinoa is cooking, preheat your grill or grill pan to medium-high heat.

3- In a large bowl, toss the sliced red bell pepper, zucchini, and red onion with olive oil. Season with salt and pepper.

4- Grill the vegetables until they have grill marks and are tender, about 5-7 minutes per side. Add the cherry tomatoes to the grill for the last 2-3 minutes, just until they start to soften.

5- In a large serving bowl, fluff the cooked quinoa with a fork. Add the grilled vegetables on top.

6- Sprinkle crumbled feta cheese over the quinoa and vegetables.

7- Tear the fresh basil leaves and scatter them on top.

8- Drizzle with balsamic glaze if desired.

9- Serve the quinoa with grilled vegetables and feta as a main dish or a side dish. Enjoy!

Nutritional Information (per serving):

Calories: 350-400

Protein: 10-12g

Fat: 15-18g

Carbohydrates: 45-50g

Fiber: 6-8g

Sugars: 4-6g

Glycemic Index (GI): Quinoa is considered a low-GI food, which means it has a minimal impact on blood sugar levels. The GI of this dish may vary depending on the specific ingredients used. To determine a precise GI value, consult a GI database or a healthcare professional.

Spelt with Sun-Dried Tomatoes and Pesto

- *Difficulty Level:* ☐☐
- *Preparation Time: 15 minutes*
- *Cooking Time: 25-30 minutes*
- *Cooking Skill: Intermediate*

Ingredients for Two:

- *1 cup pearled spelt*
- *2 cups water or vegetable broth*
- *1/2 cup sun-dried tomatoes, not in oil, thinly sliced*
- *2 tablespoons pesto sauce*
- *2 tablespoons pine nuts*
- *1/4 cup grated Parmesan cheese*
- *2 tablespoons olive oil*
- *Salt and pepper to taste*
- *Fresh basil leaves for garnish (optional)*

Instructions:

1- *Rinse the pearled spelt thoroughly in a fine mesh strainer. In a medium saucepan, combine the spelt and water (or vegetable broth). Bring to a boil, then reduce the heat to low, cover, and simmer for about 25-30 minutes, or until the spelt is tender and the liquid is absorbed. If needed, add more liquid and cook for an additional 5-10 minutes.*

2- *While the spelt is cooking, soak the sun-dried tomatoes in warm water for 10-15 minutes to soften them. Drain and thinly slice them.*

3- *In a small pan, lightly toast the pine nuts over medium-low heat until they are golden brown. Be careful not to burn them.*

4- *In a large serving bowl, combine the cooked spelt, sun-dried tomatoes, pesto sauce, toasted pine nuts, and grated Parmesan cheese.*

5- *Drizzle with olive oil and gently toss the ingredients to combine. Season with salt and pepper to taste.*

6- *Garnish with fresh basil leaves if desired.*

7- *Serve the spelt with sun-dried tomatoes and pesto as a main dish or a side dish for two. Enjoy!*

Nutritional Information (per serving):

Calories: 350-400

Protein: 10-12g

Fat: 15-18g

Carbohydrates: 45-50g

Fiber: 6-8g

Sugars: 4-6g

Glycemic Index (GI): Pearled spelt is considered a low-GI grain, which means it has a minimal impact on blood sugar levels. The GI of this dish may vary depending on the specific ingredients used.

Orzo with Chickpeas and Black Olives

- *Difficulty Level:* ☐☐
- *Preparation Time: 10 minutes*
- *Cooking Time: 15-20 minutes*
- *Cooking Skill: Easy*

Ingredients for Two:

- *1 cup orzo pasta*
- *1 cup canned chickpeas, drained and rinsed*
- *1/2 cup black olives, pitted and sliced*
- *2 tablespoons olive oil*
- *2 cloves garlic, minced*
- *1/2 teaspoon dried oregano*
- *Juice of 1 lemon*
- *Salt and pepper to taste*
- *Fresh parsley for garnish (optional)*

Instructions:

1- *Cook the orzo pasta according to the package instructions until al dente. Drain and set aside.*

2- *In a large skillet, heat the olive oil over medium heat. Add the minced garlic and cook for about 1 minute until fragrant.*

3- *Add the cooked orzo, chickpeas, and black olives to the skillet. Stir well to combine.*

4- *Season with dried oregano, lemon juice, salt, and pepper. Adjust the seasoning to your taste.*

5- *Cook for an additional 2-3 minutes, allowing the ingredients to heat through.*

6- *Serve the orzo with chickpeas and black olives hot, garnished with fresh parsley if desired.*

Nutritional Information (per serving):

Calories: 400-450
Protein: 12-14g
Fat: 10-12g
Carbohydrates: 70-75g
Fiber: 7-9g
Sugars: 3-4g

Glycemic Index (GI): Orzo pasta typically has a moderate GI, which means it can moderately affect blood sugar levels. The addition of chickpeas and olives provides fiber and healthy fats, which can help stabilize blood sugar.

Whole Wheat Couscous with Dried Fruits and Herbs

- *Difficulty Level:* ☐☐
- *Preparation Time: 15 minutes*
- *Cooking Time: 5 minutes*
- *Cooking Skill: Easy*

Ingredients for Two:

- *1 cup whole wheat couscous*
- *1 cup vegetable broth or water*
- *1/4 cup dried apricots, chopped*
- *1/4 cup dried cranberries or raisins*
- *2 tablespoons chopped fresh mint*
- *2 tablespoons chopped fresh parsley*
- *1/4 cup mixed nuts (e.g., almonds, walnuts), toasted and chopped*
- *2 tablespoons olive oil*
- *Juice of 1 lemon*
- *Salt and pepper to taste*

Instructions:

1- *In a saucepan, bring the vegetable broth or water to a boil.*

2- *Place the whole wheat couscous in a heatproof bowl. Pour the boiling broth over the couscous. Cover the bowl with a lid or plastic wrap and let it sit for 5 minutes.*

3- *Fluff the couscous with a fork to separate the grains.*

4- *In a large bowl, combine the cooked couscous, chopped dried apricots, dried cranberries (or raisins), fresh mint, fresh parsley, and mixed nuts.*

5- *Drizzle olive oil and lemon juice over the couscous mixture and season with salt and pepper to taste.*

6- *Toss all the ingredients together until well combined.*

7- *Serve the whole wheat couscous with dried fruits and herbs as a flavorful and nutritious side dish.*

Nutritional Information (per serving):

Calories: 350-400

Protein: 9-11g

Fat: 13-15g

Carbohydrates: 50-55g

Fiber: 8-10g

Sugars: 15-18g

Glycemic Index (GI): Whole wheat couscous typically has a moderate GI, which means it can moderately affect blood sugar levels. The addition of dried fruits and nuts may influence the GI slightly. For precise GI values, consult a GI database or a healthcare professional.

Bulgur with Tomatoes, Cucumbers, and Parsley

- *Difficulty Level: ☐*
- *Preparation Time: 15 minutes*
- *Cooking Time: 0 minutes*
- *Cooking Skill: Easy*

Ingredients for Two:

- *1 cup bulgur*
- *2 cups boiling water*
- *2 medium tomatoes, diced*
- *1 cucumber, diced*
- *1/4 cup fresh parsley, chopped*
- *2 tablespoons fresh mint, chopped*
- *2 tablespoons olive oil*
- *Juice of 1 lemon*
- *Salt and pepper to taste*

Instructions:

1- *Place the bulgur in a heatproof bowl. Pour the boiling water over the bulgur. Cover the bowl with a lid or plastic wrap and let it sit for about 15 minutes or until the water is absorbed.*

2- *Fluff the cooked bulgur with a fork to separate the grains and allow it to cool to room temperature.*

3- *In a large bowl, combine the cooked bulgur, diced tomatoes, diced cucumber, chopped fresh parsley, and fresh mint.*

4- Drizzle olive oil and lemon juice over the mixture and season with salt and pepper to taste.

5- Toss all the ingredients together until well combined.

6- Serve the bulgur salad with tomatoes, cucumbers, and parsley as a refreshing and nutritious side dish.

Nutritional Information (per serving):

Calories: 300-350

Protein: 6-8g

Fat: 10-12g

Carbohydrates: 50-55g

Fiber: 12-15g

Sugars: 3-4g

Glycemic Index (GI): Bulgur typically has a moderate GI, meaning it can moderately affect blood sugar levels. The addition of fresh vegetables and herbs may influence the GI slightly. For precise GI values, consult a GI database or a healthcare professional.

Amaranth with Avocado and Citrus

- Difficulty Level: ☐
- Preparation Time: 15 minutes
- Cooking Time: 20 minutes
- Cooking Skill: Easy

Ingredients for Two:

- 1/2 cup amaranth
- 1 cup water or vegetable broth
- 1 avocado, diced
- 1 grapefruit, segmented
- 1 orange, segmented
- 1/4 cup fresh cilantro, chopped
- 2 tablespoons olive oil
- Juice of 1 lime
- Salt and pepper to taste

Instructions:

1- Rinse the amaranth under cold water in a fine-mesh strainer.

2- In a medium saucepan, combine the amaranth and water (or vegetable broth). Bring it to a boil, then reduce the heat, cover, and simmer for about 20 minutes or until the liquid is absorbed.

3- Once the amaranth is cooked, let it cool to room temperature.

4- In a large bowl, combine the cooked amaranth, diced avocado, grapefruit segments, orange segments, and chopped fresh cilantro.

5- In a separate small bowl, whisk together the olive oil and lime juice. Season with salt and pepper.

6- Drizzle the dressing over the salad and gently toss to combine.

7- Serve the amaranth salad with avocado and citrus segments for a refreshing and nutrient-rich dish.

Nutritional Information (per serving):

Calories: 250-300

Protein: 6-8g

Fat: 12-14g

Carbohydrates: 30-35g

Fiber: 7-10g

Sugars: 10-12g

Glycemic Index (GI): Amaranth has a low to moderate GI, depending on the cooking method and preparation. The addition of avocados and citrus may influence the overall GI slightly..

Millet with Zucchini and Cherry Tomatoes

- Difficulty Level: ☐
- Preparation Time: 15 minutes
- Cooking Time: 25 minutes
- Cooking Skill: Easy

Ingredients for Two:

- 1 cup millet
- 2 cups water or vegetable broth
- 2 medium zucchinis, diced
- 1 cup cherry tomatoes, halved
- 2 cloves garlic, minced
- 2 tablespoons olive oil
- 1/4 cup fresh basil, chopped
- Juice of 1 lemon
- Salt and pepper to taste

Instructions:

1. Rinse the millet under cold water in a fine-mesh strainer.

2. In a medium saucepan, combine the millet and water (or vegetable broth). Bring it to a boil, then reduce the heat, cover, and simmer for about 20-25 minutes, or until the liquid is absorbed and the millet is tender. Remove from heat and let it sit, covered, for a few minutes.

3. While the millet is cooking, heat the olive oil in a large skillet over medium-high heat. Add the minced garlic and sauté for about 1 minute until fragrant.

4. Add the diced zucchinis and halved cherry tomatoes to the skillet. Sauté for about 5-7 minutes, or until they are tender and slightly caramelized. Season with salt and pepper.

5. In a large bowl, combine the cooked millet, sautéed zucchinis, cherry tomatoes, and fresh basil. Drizzle

   the lemon juice over the mixture.

6. Toss everything gently to combine and adjust the seasoning with salt and pepper, if needed.

7. Serve the millet with zucchini and cherry tomatoes for a delicious and nutritious meal.

Nutritional Information (per serving):

Calories: 300-350

Protein: 8-10g

Fat: 10-12g

Carbohydrates: 45-50g

Fiber: 7-10g

Sugars: 4-6g

Glycemic Index (GI): Millet generally has a low GI, which makes it a good choice for managing blood sugar levels. The addition of zucchinis and cherry tomatoes should maintain a low GI for this dish. To determine precise GI values, refer to a GI database or consult a healthcare professional.

Millet with Zucchini and Cherry Tomatoes

- *Difficulty Level:* ☐
- *Preparation Time: 15 minutes*
- *Cooking Time: 25 minutes*
- *Cooking Skill: Easy*

Ingredients for Two:

- *1 cup millet*
- *2 cups water or vegetable broth*
- *2 medium zucchinis, diced*
- *1 cup cherry tomatoes, halved*
- *2 cloves garlic, minced*
- *2 tablespoons olive oil*
- *1/4 cup fresh basil, chopped*
- *Juice of 1 lemon*
- *Salt and pepper to taste*

Instructions:

1- *Rinse the millet under cold water in a fine-mesh strainer.*

2- *In a medium saucepan, combine the millet and water (or vegetable broth). Bring it to a boil, then reduce the heat, cover, and simmer for about 20-25 minutes, or until the liquid is absorbed and the millet is tender. Remove from heat and let it sit, covered, for a few minutes.*

3- *While the millet is cooking, heat the olive oil in a large skillet over medium-high heat. Add the minced garlic and sauté for about 1 minute until fragrant.*

4- *Add the diced zucchinis and halved cherry tomatoes to the skillet. Sauté for about 5-7 minutes, or until they are tender and slightly caramelized. Season with salt and pepper.*

5- *In a large bowl, combine the cooked millet, sautéed zucchinis, cherry tomatoes, and fresh basil. Drizzle the lemon juice over the mixture.*

6- *Toss everything gently to combine and adjust the seasoning with salt and pepper, if needed.*

7- *Serve the millet with zucchini and cherry tomatoes for a delicious and nutritious meal.*

Nutritional Information (per serving):

Calories: 300-350

Protein: 8-10g

Fat: 10-12g

Carbohydrates: 45-50g

Fiber: 7-10g

Sugars: 4-6g

Glycemic Index (GI): Millet generally has a low GI, which makes it a good choice for managing blood sugar levels. The addition of zucchinis and cherry tomatoes should maintain a low GI for this dish.

Quinoa with Chickpea Curry and Vegetables

- *Difficulty Level:* ☐☐
- *Preparation Time: 15 minutes*
- *Cooking Time: 25 minutes*
- *Cooking Skill: Intermediate*

Ingredients for Two:

- *1 cup quinoa*
- *2 cups vegetable broth or water*
- *1 can (15 oz) chickpeas, drained and rinsed*
- *1 small onion, finely chopped*
- *2 cloves garlic, minced*
- *1 tablespoon olive oil*
- *1 can (14 oz) diced tomatoes*
- *1 cup mixed vegetables (e.g., bell peppers, zucchini, or carrots), diced*
- *2 teaspoons curry powder*
- *1/2 teaspoon ground cumin*
- *1/2 teaspoon ground coriander*
- *1/4 teaspoon cayenne pepper (adjust to taste)*
- *Salt and pepper to taste*
- *Fresh cilantro leaves for garnish (optional)*

Instructions:

1- *Rinse the quinoa under cold water using a fine mesh strainer.*

2- *In a saucepan, bring the vegetable broth (or water) to a boil. Add the rinsed quinoa, reduce the heat to low, cover, and simmer for about 15 minutes or until the quinoa is cooked and the liquid is absorbed. Remove from heat and let it rest, covered, for 5 minutes before fluffing it with a fork.*

3- *While the quinoa is cooking, heat olive oil in a large skillet over medium heat. Add the chopped onion and sauté for 3-4 minutes until it becomes translucent.*

4- *Add the minced garlic and sauté for an additional 30 seconds until fragrant.*

5- *Stir in the diced tomatoes, mixed vegetables, chickpeas, and all the spices (curry powder, ground cumin, ground coriander, cayenne pepper, salt, and pepper). Simmer for about 10-12 minutes, or until the vegetables are tender.*

6- *Serve the chickpea curry over the cooked quinoa.*

7- *Garnish with fresh cilantro leaves if desired.*

Nutritional Information (per serving):

Calories: 400-450
Protein: 15-18g
Fat: 10-12g
Carbohydrates: 65-70g
Fiber: 10-12g
Sugars: 8-10g

Glycemic Index (GI): Quinoa has a low GI, which can help stabilize blood sugar levels. Chickpeas and vegetables also contribute to keeping the

Wild Rice with Shiitake Mushrooms

- *Difficulty Level: ☐☐*
- *Preparation Time: 10 minutes*
- *Cooking Time: 45 minutes*
- *Cooking Skill: Intermediate*

Ingredients for Two:

- *1 cup wild rice*
- *2 cups vegetable broth or water*

- 8 oz (about 2 cups) shiitake mushrooms, sliced
- 1 small onion, finely chopped
- 2 cloves garlic, minced
- 2 tablespoons olive oil
- 2 tablespoons fresh parsley , chopped
- Salt and pepper to taste

Instructions:

1- Rinse the wild rice under cold water using a fine mesh strainer.

2- In a saucepan, bring the vegetable broth (or water) to a boil. Add the rinsed wild rice, reduce the heat to low, cover, and simmer for about 45 minutes or until the rice is tender and the liquid is absorbed. Remove from heat and let it rest, covered, for 5 minutes before fluffing it with a fork.

3- While the rice is cooking, heat olive oil in a large skillet over medium heat. Add the chopped onion and sauté for 3-4 minutes until it becomes translucent.

4- Add the minced garlic and sauté for an additional 30 seconds until fragrant.

5- Stir in the sliced shiitake mushrooms and continue to sauté for about 5-7 minutes until the mushrooms are tender and slightly browned. Season with salt and pepper to taste.

6- Combine the cooked wild rice and sautéed shiitake mushrooms in a serving bowl, mixing them together.

7- Garnish with fresh chopped parsley.

Nutritional Information (per serving):

Calories: 350-400

Protein: 9-11g

Fat: 7-9g

Carbohydrates: 65-70g

Fiber: 6-8g

Sugars: 3-5g

Glycemic Index (GI): Wild rice typically has a lower GI compared to white rice, which can help maintain steady blood sugar levels. The addition of shiitake mushrooms and vegetables contributes to keeping the GI relatively low. If you have specific dietary concerns, consult a healthcare professional for guidance.

LEGUMES

Chickpea Hummus with Raw Vegetables

- Difficulty Level: ☐
- Preparation Time: 10 minutes
- Cooking Time: 0 minutes
- Cooking Skill: Easy

Ingredients for Two:

For the Hummus:

- 1 can (15 oz) chickpeas, drained and rinsed
- 2-3 tablespoons tahini (sesame paste)

- *2 cloves garlic, minced*
- *2 tablespoons lemon juice*
- *2 tablespoons olive oil*
- *1/2 teaspoon ground cumin*
- *Salt and pepper to taste*
- *Water, as needed to reach desired consistency*

For the Raw Vegetables:

1- *A mix of raw vegetables such as carrot sticks, cucumber slices, bell pepper strips, and celery sticks*

2- *Instructions:*

3- *In a food processor, combine the drained and rinsed chickpeas, tahini, minced garlic, lemon juice, olive oil, ground cumin, salt, and pepper.*

4- *Blend the ingredients until smooth. If the hummus is too thick, you can add a little water to achieve your preferred consistency. Continue to blend until you reach the desired smoothness.*

5- *Taste the hummus and adjust the seasonings if necessary. You can add more lemon juice, salt, or other seasonings to suit your taste.*

6- *Serve the freshly made hummus with a selection of raw vegetables for dipping. Carrot sticks, cucumber slices, bell pepper strips, and celery sticks are popular choices, but feel free to use your favorites.*

Nutritional Information (per serving):

Calories: 150-200

Protein: 4-6g

Fat: 8-10g

Carbohydrates: 15-20g

Fiber: 5-7g

Sugars: 2-4g

Glycemic Index (GI): Chickpeas have a moderate GI. When combined with raw vegetables, this dish is relatively low on the GI scale, making it a healthy and balanced snack option. If you have specific dietary concerns, consult a healthcare professional for guidance.

Sautéed Black Beans with Bell Peppers and Onions

- *Difficulty Level: ☐☐*
- *Preparation Time: 15 minutes*
- *Cooking Time: 15 minutes*
- *Cooking Skill: Easy*

Ingredients for Two:

- *1 can (15 oz) black beans, drained and rinsed*
- *1 red bell pepper, thinly sliced*
- *1 yellow bell pepper, thinly sliced*
- *1 medium onion, thinly sliced*
- *2 cloves garlic, minced*
- *2 tablespoons olive oil*
- *1 teaspoon ground cumin*
- *1 teaspoon chili powder (adjust to taste)*
- *Salt and pepper to taste*
- *Fresh cilantro leaves, for garnish (optional)*
- *Lime wedges, for serving*

Instructions:

1- *Heat olive oil in a large skillet over medium heat. Add the sliced onions and* cook until they become translucent and slightly caramelized, about 3-5 minutes.

2- Add the minced garlic and cook for another 1-2 minutes until fragrant.

3- Stir in the sliced red and yellow bell peppers and sauté for about 5-7 minutes or until they become tender and slightly charred.

4- Add the drained and rinsed black beans to the skillet and sprinkle the ground cumin and chili powder over the mixture.

5- Continue to sauté the ingredients for another 2-3 minutes, allowing the flavors to meld and the beans to heat through.

6- Season with salt and pepper to taste.

7- Serve the sautéed black beans, bell peppers, and onions hot. Garnish with fresh cilantro leaves, if desired, and serve with lime wedges on the side for an extra burst of flavor.

Nutritional Information (per serving):

Calories: 300-350

Protein: 10-12g

Fat: 8-10g

Carbohydrates: 45-50g

Fiber: 15-18g

Sugars: 7-9g

Glycemic Index (GI): Black beans have a low to moderate GI, depending on the cooking method. This dish is rich in fiber and provides steady energy, making it a suitable option for those

seeking balanced nutrition. As always, consult a healthcare professional for specific dietary recommendations.

Curried Lentils with Spinach

- Difficulty Level: ☐☐
- Preparation Time: 10 minutes
- Cooking Time: 25 minutes
- Cooking Skill: Easy

Ingredients for Two:

- 1 cup dried green or brown lentils
- 2 1/2 cups water
- 1 small onion, finely chopped
- 2 cloves garlic, minced
- 1 tablespoon olive oil
- 1 tablespoon curry powder
- 1/2 teaspoon ground cumin
- 1/2 teaspoon ground coriander
- 1/4 teaspoon turmeric
- 1/4 teaspoon cayenne pepper (adjust to taste)
- 1 can (14 oz) diced tomatoes
- 4 cups fresh spinach leaves
- Salt and pepper to taste
- Lemon wedges, for serving (optional)

Instructions:

1- Rinse the lentils under cold water and drain them.

2- In a medium saucepan, heat the olive oil over medium heat. Add the chopped onion and sauté for 2-3 minutes until it becomes translucent.

3- Stir in the minced garlic and continue cooking for another minute until fragrant.

4- Add the curry powder, ground cumin, ground coriander, turmeric, and cayenne pepper to the onion and garlic mixture. Sauté for another 1-2 minutes to release the flavors of the spices.

5- Pour in the diced tomatoes and mix well with the spice mixture. Allow the mixture to simmer for about 5 minutes, or until it thickens slightly.

6- Add the rinsed lentils and water to the saucepan. Bring the mixture to a boil, then reduce the heat to low. Cover and simmer for approximately 15-20 minutes, or until the lentils are tender and most of the liquid is absorbed.

7- Stir in the fresh spinach leaves and cook for an additional 3-5 minutes, or until the spinach wilts and incorporates into the lentils.

8- Season with salt and pepper to taste.

9- Serve the curried lentils with spinach hot, garnished with lemon wedges if desired. The lemon adds a fresh citrusy touch to the dish.

Nutritional Information (per serving):

- Calories: 300-350
- Protein: 15-17g
- Fat: 5-7g
- Carbohydrates: 50-55g
- Fiber: 15-18g
- Sugars: 4-6g

Glycemic Index (GI): Lentils have a low GI, which helps maintain stable blood sugar levels.

The addition of spinach and tomatoes makes this a balanced, nutritious meal. However, individual responses may vary, so consult a healthcare professional for specific dietary guidance.

Chickpea Frittata with Zucchini and Tomatoes

- Difficulty Level: ☐☐
- Preparation Time: 10 minutes
- Cooking Time: 20 minutes
- Cooking Skill: Easy

Ingredients for Two:

- 1 can (14 oz) chickpeas, drained and rinsed
- 1 small zucchini, sliced into thin rounds
- 1 cup cherry tomatoes, halved
- 1/2 onion, finely chopped
- 4 large eggs
- 2 tablespoons olive oil
- 1/2 teaspoon ground cumin
- 1/2 teaspoon ground paprika
- Salt and pepper to taste
- Fresh parsley, for garnish (optional)

Instructions:

1- In a large ovenproof skillet, heat the olive oil over medium heat.

2- Add the chopped onion and sliced zucchini. Sauté for about 5 minutes until the zucchini begins to soften and the onions become translucent.

3- Stir in the halved cherry tomatoes and continue cooking for another 2-3 minutes, allowing them to soften slightly.

4- Add the chickpeas to the skillet and season with ground cumin, ground paprika, salt, and pepper. Cook for an additional 2 minutes, ensuring the chickpeas are heated through.

5- In a separate bowl, beat the eggs and then pour them over the chickpea and vegetable mixture in the skillet.

6- Allow the frittata to cook undisturbed for about 5-7 minutes on medium-low heat, or until the edges set.

7- Preheat your broiler.

8- Place the skillet under the broiler for about 3-5 minutes, or until the frittata is set, puffed, and slightly browned on top.

9- Carefully remove the skillet from the broiler (use oven mitts), and garnish the chickpea frittata with fresh parsley if desired.

Nutritional Information (per serving):

Calories: 300-350

Protein: 14-16g

Fat: 15-18g

Carbohydrates: 26-30g

Fiber: 6-8g

Sugars: 4-6g

Glycemic Index (GI): Chickpeas have a low GI, which helps maintain stable blood sugar levels. This frittata is a balanced and nutritious meal. However, individual responses may vary, so consult a healthcare professional for specific dietary guidance.

- Difficulty Level: ☐☐
- Preparation Time: 15 minutes
- Cooking Time: 0 minutes
- Cooking Skill: Easy

Ingredients for Two:

- 1 can (14 oz) mixed beans (such as kidney beans, black beans, and cannellini beans), drained and rinsed
- 1/2 red onion, finely chopped
- 1/2 cup fresh basil leaves, chopped
- 2 tablespoons extra-virgin olive oil
- 2 tablespoons red wine vinegar
- Salt and pepper to taste

Instructions:

1- In a large mixing bowl, combine the mixed beans, finely chopped red onion, and fresh basil leaves.

2- In a separate small bowl, whisk together the extra-virgin olive oil, red wine vinegar, salt, and pepper to create the dressing.

3- Pour the dressing over the mixed beans and toss the salad well to ensure all the ingredients are evenly coated.

4- Let the salad sit for about 15 minutes to allow the flavors to meld.

5- Before serving, give the salad a final toss and adjust the seasoning with additional salt and pepper if needed.

6- Garnish the salad with some extra basil leaves.

7- Serve your mixed bean salad as a healthy and flavorful side dish.

Nutritional Information (per serving):

1- Calories: 250-300
2- Protein: 8-10g
3- Fat: 10-12g
4- Carbohydrates: 30-35g
5- Fiber: 8-10g
6- Sugars: 2-3g

7- Glycemic Index (GI): The glycemic index for mixed beans can vary, but in general, they have a relatively low GI, making this salad a balanced choice for maintaining stable blood sugar levels. However, individual responses may vary, so consult a healthcare professional for specific dietary guidance.

8- Lentil Frittata with Sun-Dried Tomatoes

9- Difficulty Level: ☐☐
10- Preparation Time: 20 minutes
11- Cooking Time: 15 minutes
12- Cooking Skill: Easy

13- Ingredients for Two:

14- 1/2 cup dried green or brown lentils
15- 4 large eggs
16- 1/4 cup sun-dried tomatoes, chopped
17- 1/4 cup crumbled feta cheese
18- 1/4 cup fresh spinach, chopped
19- 2 cloves garlic, minced
20- 1/2 teaspoon dried oregano
21- Salt and pepper to taste
22- 2 tablespoons olive oil

23- Instructions:

24- Cook the lentils: Rinse the lentils and cook them according to the package instructions until they are tender. Drain and set aside.

25- Preheat the oven to 350°F (175°C).

26- In a mixing bowl, whisk the eggs.

27- Add the cooked lentils, sun-dried tomatoes, feta cheese, fresh spinach, minced garlic, dried oregano, salt, and pepper to the eggs. Mix well to combine all the ingredients.

28- Heat the olive oil in an oven-safe skillet over medium heat.

29- Pour the lentil mixture into the skillet and cook for about 3-4 minutes or until the edges start to set.

30- Transfer the skillet to the preheated oven and bake for about 10-12 minutes, or until the frittata is set and slightly golden on top.

31- Remove the skillet from the oven, and let the frittata cool for a few minutes.

32- Slice the frittata into wedges and serve.

33- Enjoy your lentil frittata with sun-dried tomatoes as a nutritious and flavorful meal!

Nutritional Information (per serving):

Calories: 250-300

Protein: 14-16g

Fat: 12-14g

Carbohydrates: 20-25g

Fiber: 5-7g

Sugars: 2-3g

Glycemic Index (GI): Lentils have a low glycemic index, and this frittata is a balanced choice for maintaining stable blood sugar levels. However, individual responses may vary, so consult a healthcare professional for specific dietary guidance.

Roasted Sweet Potatoes with Spiced Chickpeas

- *Difficulty Level:* ☐☐
- *Preparation Time: 15 minutes*
- *Cooking Time: 30-35 minutes*
- *Cooking Skill: Easy*

Ingredients for Two:

For Roasted Sweet Potatoes:

- *2 medium sweet potatoes, peeled and cut into 1-inch cubes*
- *2 tablespoons olive oil*
- *1 teaspoon ground cumin*
- *1 teaspoon paprika*
- *Salt and pepper to taste*

For Spiced Chickpeas:

- *1 can (15 oz) chickpeas, drained and rinsed*
- *1 tablespoon olive oil*
- *1/2 teaspoon ground cumin*
- *1/2 teaspoon ground coriander*

- *1/2 teaspoon smoked paprika*
- *Salt and pepper to taste*

For Garnish:

- *Fresh cilantro or parsley, chopped*
- *Greek yogurt (optional)*

Instructions:

1- *Preheat your oven to 425°F (220°C).*

2- *In a mixing bowl, combine the sweet potato cubes with olive oil, ground cumin, paprika, salt, and pepper. Toss until the sweet potato pieces are evenly coated.*

3- *Spread the seasoned sweet potato cubes on a baking sheet in a single layer. Roast them in the preheated oven for about 20-25 minutes, or until they are tender and slightly crispy. Stir or flip them halfway through for even cooking.*

4- *While the sweet potatoes are roasting, prepare the spiced chickpeas. In another bowl, toss the chickpeas with olive oil, ground cumin, ground coriander, smoked paprika, salt, and pepper.*

5- *Once the sweet potatoes are almost done, add the seasoned chickpeas to the same baking sheet. Roast for an additional 10-12 minutes, or until the chickpeas are slightly crispy.*

6- *Remove from the oven, garnish with chopped cilantro or parsley, and add a dollop of Greek yogurt if desired.*

7- Serve the roasted sweet potatoes and spiced chickpeas hot as a delicious and satisfying meal.

Nutritional Information (per serving):

Calories: 350-400

Protein: 8-10g

Fat: 14-16g

Carbohydrates: 50-55g

Fiber: 10-12g

Sugars: 10-12g

Glycemic Index (GI): Sweet potatoes have a moderate GI, and chickpeas have a low GI. This dish offers a balanced mix of carbohydrates and protein for sustained energy. However, individual responses may vary, so consult a healthcare professional for specific dietary guidance.

Couscous and Grilled Vegetable Salad with Chickpeas

- Difficulty Level: ☐☐
- Preparation Time: 20 minutes
- Cooking Time: 10 minutes
- Cooking Skill: Easy

Ingredients for Two:

For the Salad:

- 1 cup couscous
- 1 1/4 cups vegetable broth or water
- 1 can (15 oz) chickpeas, drained and rinsed
- 1 red bell pepper, sliced
- 1 zucchini, sliced into rounds
- 1 small red onion, cut into wedges
- 1 cup cherry tomatoes
- 1/4 cup fresh parsley, chopped
- 1/4 cup fresh mint, chopped
- Juice of 1 lemon
- 2 tablespoons olive oil
- Salt and pepper to taste

For the Dressing:

- 3 tablespoons olive oil
- 2 tablespoons balsamic vinegar
- 1 garlic clove, minced
- 1 teaspoon Dijon mustard
- Salt and pepper to taste

Instructions:

1- Prepare the couscous by boiling the vegetable broth or water. Once it boils, add the couscous, cover, and remove from heat. Let it sit for 5 minutes, then fluff it with a fork.

2- Heat your grill to medium-high heat.

3- In a large bowl, toss the sliced red bell pepper, zucchini rounds, red onion wedges, and cherry tomatoes with olive oil, salt, and pepper.

4- Grill the vegetables on each side until they are tender and have grill marks. This typically takes 2-4 minutes for the zucchini, red bell pepper, and onion and about 1-2 minutes for the cherry tomatoes.

5- While the vegetables are grilling, prepare the dressing. In a small bowl, whisk together the olive oil, balsamic vinegar, minced garlic, Dijon mustard, salt, and pepper. Set aside.

6- In a large serving bowl, combine the cooked couscous, grilled vegetables, chickpeas, chopped parsley, and mint.

7- Drizzle the lemon juice over the salad, then pour the dressing and toss gently to combine.

8- Taste and adjust the seasoning with additional salt and pepper if needed.

9- Serve the couscous and grilled vegetable salad with chickpeas warm or at room temperature.

Nutritional Information (per serving):

Calories: 350-400

Protein: 10-12g

Fat: 12-14g

Carbohydrates: 50-55g

Fiber: 10-12g

Sugars: 8-10g

Glycemic Index (GI): Couscous has a moderate GI, while chickpeas have a low GI. This dish offers a good balance of carbohydrates, fiber, and protein for sustained energy. However, individual responses may vary, so consult a healthcare professional for specific dietary guidance.

Braised Chickpeas with Tomatoes and Kale

- Difficulty Level: ☐☐
- Preparation Time: 15 minutes
- Cooking Time: 40 minutes
- Cooking Skill: Intermediate

Ingredients for Two:

- 1 can (15 oz) chickpeas, drained and rinsed
- 2 cups kale, chopped
- 1 can (14 oz) diced tomatoes
- 1 onion, chopped
- 2 cloves garlic, minced
- 1 teaspoon olive oil
- 1 teaspoon ground cumin
- 1/2 teaspoon paprika
- 1/4 teaspoon red pepper flakes (adjust to taste)
- Salt and black pepper to taste
- 1/2 cup vegetable broth
- Fresh parsley for garnish (optional)

Instructions:

1- In a large skillet, heat the olive oil over medium heat. Add the chopped onion and cook for about 5 minutes, or until it becomes translucent.

2- Stir in the minced garlic and cook for another 30 seconds until fragrant.

3- Add the ground cumin, paprika, and red pepper flakes. Stir to coat the onion and garlic with the spices.

4- Pour in the diced tomatoes and their juices. Stir well.

5- Add the drained and rinsed chickpeas to the skillet. Mix them with the tomato mixture.

6- Season with salt and black pepper to taste.

7- Pour the vegetable broth into the skillet and bring everything to a simmer. Let it cook for about 20-25 minutes, stirring occasionally, until the mixture thickens and the flavors meld together.

8- About 5 minutes before the end of the cooking time, add the chopped kale to the skillet. Stir it into the chickpea and tomato mixture and let it cook until it's wilted and tender.

9- Taste and adjust the seasoning if necessary.

10- Serve the braised chickpeas with tomatoes and kale in individual plates, garnished with fresh parsley if desired.

Nutritional Information (per serving):

Calories: 300-350

Protein: 10-12g

Fat: 4-6g

Carbohydrates: 50-55g

Fiber: 15-20g

Sugars: 8-10g

Glycemic Index (GI): Chickpeas have a low GI, which makes this dish a good option for maintaining stable blood sugar levels. The kale adds extra fiber and nutrients. However, individual responses may vary, so consult a healthcare professional for specific dietary guidance.

MEAT FIRST COURSE

Chicken and Mushroom Risotto with Mustard

- Difficulty Level: ☐☐☐
- Preparation Time: 10 minutes
- Cooking Time: 30 minutes
- Cooking Skill: Intermediate

Ingredients for Two:

- 1 cup Arborio rice
- 2 boneless, skinless chicken breasts, cut into bite-sized pieces
- 8 oz (about 2 cups) mushrooms, sliced
- 1 small onion, finely chopped
- 2 cloves garlic, minced
- 3 cups chicken broth
- 1/2 cup white wine (optional)
- 2 tablespoons Dijon mustard
- 2 tablespoons butter
- 2 tablespoons olive oil
- Salt and black pepper to taste
- Fresh parsley, chopped, for garnish (optional)

Instructions:

1- In a large skillet or pan, heat the olive oil over medium heat. Add the chicken pieces and cook until they're no longer pink in the center. Remove the chicken from the pan and set it aside.

2- In the same pan, add the chopped onions and cook until they become translucent.

3- Add the minced garlic and cook for about 30 seconds, until fragrant.

4- Stir in the Arborio rice and cook for 2-3 minutes until the rice becomes slightly translucent at the edges.

5- If using white wine, pour it into the pan and stir until it's mostly absorbed.

6- Begin adding the chicken broth one ladle at a time. Allow the broth to be absorbed by the rice before adding more. Stir continuously and maintain a simmer.

7- After about 15 minutes, when the rice is almost tender, add the sliced mushrooms and continue adding broth.

8- Once the rice is creamy and the mushrooms are tender, stir in the cooked chicken pieces.

9- Remove the pan from the heat, and add the Dijon mustard, butter, and season with salt and black pepper. Stir well to combine.

10- Let the risotto rest for a few minutes before serving.

11- Garnish with chopped fresh parsley if desired.

Nutritional Information (per serving):

Calories: 450-500

Protein: 25-30g

Fat: 15-18g

Carbohydrates: 40-45g

Fiber: 2-4g

Sugars: 2-4g

Glycemic Index (GI): This dish typically has a medium GI due to the Arborio rice. Adding chicken, mushrooms, and mustard will help moderate the blood sugar response. Individual responses may vary, so consult a healthcare professional for specific dietary guidance.

Whole Wheat Tagliatelle with Chicken Curry and Vegetables

- Difficulty Level: ☐☐☐
- Preparation Time: 15 minutes
- Cooking Time: 25 minutes
- Cooking Skill: Intermediate

Ingredients for Two:

- 6 oz whole wheat tagliatelle pasta
- 2 boneless, skinless chicken breasts, cut into bite-sized pieces
- 1 cup mixed vegetables (e.g., bell peppers, broccoli, carrots), sliced
- 1 small onion, finely chopped
- 2 cloves garlic, minced
- 1 cup coconut milk
- 2 tablespoons curry powder
- 2 tablespoons olive oil
- Salt and black pepper to taste
- Fresh cilantro or basil, for garnish (optional)

Instructions:

1- Cook the whole wheat tagliatelle pasta according to the package instructions until al dente. Drain and set aside.

2- In a large skillet, heat the olive oil over medium heat. Add the chopped onions and cook until they become translucent.

3- Add the minced garlic and cook for about 30 seconds until fragrant.

4- Add the chicken pieces and cook until they're no longer pink in the center.

5- Stir in the mixed vegetables and cook for a few minutes until they start to soften.

6- Sprinkle the curry powder over the chicken and vegetables, and stir well to coat everything evenly.

7- Pour in the coconut milk and bring the mixture to a simmer. Let it cook for 5-7 minutes, or until the chicken is cooked through and the sauce thickens.

8- Season with salt and black pepper to taste.

9- Serve the curry over the cooked whole wheat tagliatelle pasta.

10- Garnish with fresh cilantro or basil if desired.

Nutritional Information (per serving):

Calories: 400-450

Protein: 25-30g

Fat: 15-18g

Carbohydrates: 40-45g

Fiber: 8-10g

Sugars: 3-4g

Glycemic Index (GI): This dish has a low to moderate GI depending on the amount of pasta consumed. The whole wheat pasta and fiber-rich vegetables help stabilize blood sugar levels. Individual responses may vary, so consult a healthcare professional for specific dietary guidance.

Lean Meat Lasagna with Spinach and Ricotta

- Difficulty Level: □□□
- Preparation Time: 30 minutes
- Cooking Time: 1 hour
- Cooking Skill: Intermediate

Ingredients for Two:

- 6 whole wheat lasagna noodles
- 1/2 pound lean ground beef or turkey
- 1 small onion, finely chopped
- 2 cloves garlic, minced
- 1 (14-ounce) can crushed tomatoes
- 1 teaspoon dried basil
- 1 teaspoon dried oregano
- Salt and black pepper to taste
- 1 cup fresh spinach leaves
- 1 cup low-fat ricotta cheese
- 1/2 cup shredded part-skim mozzarella cheese
- 2 tablespoons grated Parmesan cheese
- Fresh basil leaves for garnish (optional)

Instructions:

1- Cook the whole wheat lasagna noodles according to the package instructions until al dente. Drain and set aside.

2- In a large skillet, cook the lean ground meat over medium heat until browned. Drain any excess fat.

3- Add the chopped onion and minced garlic to the skillet with the meat. Cook for a few minutes until the onion becomes translucent.

4- Stir in the crushed tomatoes, dried basil, dried oregano, salt, and black pepper. Simmer for 15-20 minutes, allowing the sauce to thicken.

5- Preheat your oven to 375°F (190°C).

6- In a separate bowl, mix the fresh spinach with the ricotta cheese.

7- In a baking dish, spread a thin layer of the meat sauce.

8- Place three lasagna noodles over the sauce.

9- Spread half of the spinach and ricotta mixture over the noodles.

10- Add another layer of meat sauce over the spinach and ricotta.

11- Repeat the process by adding another layer of noodles, the remaining spinach and ricotta mixture, and another layer of meat sauce.

12- Top the lasagna with the shredded mozzarella and grated Parmesan cheese.

13- Cover the baking dish with foil and bake for 30 minutes.

14- Remove the foil and bake for an additional 15-20 minutes, or until the cheese is golden and bubbling.

15- Let the lasagna rest for a few minutes before serving.

16- Garnish with fresh basil leaves if desired.

Nutritional Information (per serving):

Calories: 450-500
Protein: 35-40g
Fat: 15-20g
Carbohydrates: 40-45g
Fiber: 5-7g
Sugars: 5-7g

Glycemic Index (GI): The use of whole wheat pasta in this lasagna helps keep the glycemic index relatively moderate. The combination of protein, fiber, and fats further aids in stabilizing blood sugar levels. Individual responses may vary, so consult a healthcare professional for specific dietary guidance.

Zucchini Noodles with Chicken and Basil Pesto

- Difficulty Level: ☐☐
- Preparation Time: 20 minutes
- Cooking Time: 15 minutes
- Cooking Skill: Intermediate

Ingredients for Two:

For the Zucchini Noodles:

- 4 medium zucchinis
- 2 tablespoons olive oil
- Salt and black pepper to taste

For the Chicken:

- 2 boneless, skinless chicken breasts
- 1 tablespoon olive oil
- 1 teaspoon Italian seasoning
- Salt and black pepper to taste

For the Basil Pesto:

- *2 cups fresh basil leaves*
- *1/3 cup grated Parmesan cheese*
- *1/4 cup pine nuts*
- *2 cloves garlic*
- *1/2 cup extra-virgin olive oil*
- *Salt and black pepper to taste*

Instructions:

1- *Spiralize the zucchinis to create zucchini noodles. You can use a spiralizer or a vegetable peeler to make thin strips.*

2- *Heat 2 tablespoons of olive oil in a large skillet over medium heat. Add the zucchini noodles and sauté for about 2-3 minutes until they are tender but still crisp. Season with salt and pepper. Transfer the zucchini noodles to a plate and cover to keep warm.*

3- *Season the chicken breasts with Italian seasoning, salt, and black pepper.*

4- *In the same skillet, add 1 tablespoon of olive oil over medium-high heat. Cook the chicken breasts for about 6-7 minutes per side until they are cooked through and no longer pink in the center. Remove the chicken from the skillet and let it rest for a few minutes before slicing it into thin strips.*

5- *In a food processor, combine the basil leaves, grated Parmesan cheese, pine nuts, garlic, and a pinch of salt and pepper. Pulse until the mixture is finely chopped.*

6- *With the food processor running, slowly drizzle in the 1/2 cup of extra-virgin olive oil until the pesto is well blended.*

7- *In the same skillet, add the zucchini noodles and sliced chicken. Pour the basil pesto over them and toss until everything is well coated.*

8- *Serve the zucchini noodles and chicken with additional grated Parmesan cheese and pine nuts on top if desired.*

Nutritional Information (per serving):

Calories: 450-500

Protein: 30-35g

Fat: 35-40g

Carbohydrates: 10-15g

Fiber: 3-5g

Sugars: 5-7g

Glycemic Index (GI): The use of zucchini noodles in this dish keeps the glycemic index very low, making it a suitable option for those watching their blood sugar levels. Individual responses may vary, so consult a healthcare professional for specific dietary guidance.

Fettuccine with Lean Sausage, Bell Peppers, and Cherry Tomatoes

- *Difficulty Level: ☐☐*
- *Preparation Time: 15 minutes*
- *Cooking Time: 20 minutes*
- *Cooking Skill: Intermediate*

Ingredients for Two:

- 8 ounces (about 230g) whole wheat fettuccine
- 2 lean Italian sausages, casing removed
- 1 red bell pepper, thinly sliced
- 1 yellow bell pepper, thinly sliced
- 1 cup cherry tomatoes, halved
- 2 cloves garlic, minced
- 1/4 teaspoon red pepper flakes (optional, for some heat)
- 2 tablespoons olive oil
- Salt and black pepper to taste
- Fresh basil leaves for garnish

Instructions:

1- Cook the fettuccine according to the package instructions until al dente. Drain and set aside.

2- In a large skillet, heat 1 tablespoon of olive oil over medium-high heat. Add the sausage meat and cook, breaking it into small pieces with a spatula, until browned and cooked through. Remove the sausage from the skillet and set it aside.

3- In the same skillet, add the remaining 1 tablespoon of olive oil. Add the sliced red and yellow bell peppers and sauté for about 4-5 minutes until they start to soften.

4- Stir in the minced garlic and red pepper flakes (if using) and sauté for another minute until fragrant.

5- Add the halved cherry tomatoes and cook for about 3-4 minutes, or until they begin to soften and release their juices.

6- Return the cooked sausage to the skillet and toss to combine with the vegetables.

7- Add the cooked fettuccine to the skillet and gently toss everything together. Season with salt and black pepper to taste.

8- Serve the fettuccine with a garnish of fresh basil leaves.

Nutritional Information (per serving):

Calories: 450-500
Protein: 18-20g
Fat: 16-18g
Carbohydrates: 50-55g
Fiber: 8-10g
Sugars: 7-9g

Glycemic Index (GI): The use of whole wheat fettuccine in this dish may help moderate the glycemic response compared to traditional pasta. However, individual responses may vary, so consult a healthcare professional for specific dietary guidance.

Tagliatelle with Pancetta, Peas, and Quail Eggs

- Difficulty Level: ☐☐
- Preparation Time: 15 minutes
- Cooking Time: 15 minutes
- Cooking Skill: Intermediate

Ingredients for Two:

- 8 ounces (about 230g) tagliatelle pasta
- 100g pancetta, diced
- 1 cup frozen peas
- 6-8 quail eggs

- *2 tablespoons grated Pecorino Romano cheese*
- *2 tablespoons heavy cream*
- *2 tablespoons butter*
- *Salt and black pepper to taste*
- *Fresh parsley leaves for garnish*

Instructions:

1- *Cook the tagliatelle pasta according to the package instructions until al dente. Drain and set aside.*

2- *While the pasta is cooking, in a large skillet, cook the diced pancetta over medium heat until it becomes crispy. Remove it from the skillet and set it aside, leaving the rendered fat in the pan.*

3- *In the same skillet, add the frozen peas and sauté for a few minutes until they are heated through.*

4- *Create small wells in the peas and crack the quail eggs into each well. Cover the skillet and cook until the quail eggs are cooked to your liking (usually about 2-3 minutes for runny yolks).*

5- *In a separate small saucepan, melt the butter over low heat, then add the heavy cream, grated Pecorino Romano cheese, salt, and black pepper. Stir until the sauce is smooth and well combined.*

6- *Toss the cooked tagliatelle pasta with the pancetta and creamy sauce.*

7- *To serve, divide the pasta among two plates and top each serving with the quail eggs and peas. Garnish with fresh parsley leaves.*

Nutritional Information (per serving):

Calories: 450-500
Protein: 15-17g
Fat: 22-24g
Carbohydrates: 40-45g
Fiber: 4-6g
Sugars: 4-6g

Glycemic Index (GI): The GI of this dish is influenced by the pasta and cream, and it may be moderate. Quail eggs are very low in carbohydrates, which can help mitigate the overall glycemic response. Individual responses may vary, so consult a healthcare professional for specific dietary guidance.

SEAFOOD FIRST COURSE

Linguine with Clams, Garlic, and Parsley

- *Difficulty Level: ☐ ☐ ☐*
- *Preparation Time: 15 minutes*
- *Cooking Time: 15 minutes*
- *Cooking Skill: Intermediate*

Ingredients for Two:

- *200g linguine pasta*
- *500g fresh clams*
- *2 cloves of garlic, minced*
- *A handful of fresh parsley, chopped*
- *1/4 cup white wine (optional)*
- *2 tablespoons olive oil*
- *Red pepper flakes (optional)*
- *Salt and black pepper to taste*

Instructions:

1- Start by cleaning the fresh clams. Place them in a bowl of cold, salted water for about 20-30 minutes. This will help them expel any sand or grit. Rinse and scrub them before using.

2- Cook the linguine pasta in a large pot of salted boiling water until al dente. Drain and set aside.

3- In a large skillet, heat the olive oil over medium heat. Add the minced garlic and cook for a minute or until it becomes fragrant.

4- Add the cleaned clams to the skillet and, if desired, pour in the white wine. Cover the skillet and let the clams steam for about 5-7 minutes or until they open. Discard any clams that do not open.

5- Once the clams are cooked, remove them from the skillet and set them aside.

6- Add the cooked linguine pasta to the skillet with the remaining clam cooking liquid. Toss to coat the pasta with the flavorful broth.

7- Return the cooked clams to the skillet, and add chopped fresh parsley. Toss everything together.

8- Season with salt, black pepper, and red pepper flakes (if you like it spicy).

9- Serve your linguine with clams immediately, garnished with additional fresh parsley and a drizzle of olive oil, if desired.

Nutritional Information (per serving):

Calories: Approximately 400-450

Protein: 20-25g

Fat: 5-8g

Carbohydrates: 65-70g

Fiber: 3-4g

Sugars: 1-2g

Glycemic Index (GI): The GI of this dish is primarily influenced by the pasta and is moderate. The presence of clams and fresh parsley may help balance the overall glycemic response. Remember that individual responses can vary, so consult a healthcare professional for specific dietary guidance.

Shrimp and Grilled Zucchini Risotto

- Difficulty Level: ☐☐☐
- Preparation Time: 10 minutes
- Cooking Time: 30 minutes
- Cooking Skill: Intermediate

Ingredients for Two:

- 1 cup Arborio rice
- 1/2 lb (about 225g) large shrimp, peeled and deveined
- 2 small zucchinis, sliced and grilled
- 1/2 cup dry white wine
- 4 cups chicken or vegetable broth, kept warm
- 1/2 cup grated Parmesan cheese
- 1 small onion, finely chopped
- 2 cloves garlic, minced
- 2 tablespoons olive oil
- 2 tablespoons butter
- Fresh basil leaves, chopped, for garnish
- Salt and black pepper to taste

Instructions:

1- Begin by grilling the zucchini slices. Brush them with a little olive oil, season with salt and pepper, and grill until they have grill marks and are tender. Set them aside.

2- In a large skillet or saucepan, heat 1 tablespoon of olive oil and 1 tablespoon of butter over medium heat.

3- Add the finely chopped onion and cook until it becomes translucent, about 3-4 minutes.

4- Stir in the minced garlic and cook for an additional minute until fragrant.

5- Add the Arborio rice and cook, stirring continuously, for about 2 minutes or until the rice is well-coated with the oil and has a slightly translucent edge.

6- Pour in the white wine and cook until it's mostly absorbed by the rice.

7- Begin adding the warm broth one ladle at a time, allowing each addition to be absorbed by the rice before adding more. Stir the risotto continuously during this process, which should take about 18-20 minutes.

8- When the risotto is almost cooked to your desired level of tenderness, gently stir in the grilled zucchini slices.

9- In a separate pan, heat the remaining tablespoon of olive oil. Sauté the shrimp for about 2-3 minutes on each side or until they turn pink and opaque.

10- Once the risotto is cooked to your liking, remove it from the heat, stir in the grated Parmesan cheese, and season with salt and black pepper to taste.

11- Serve the risotto on plates, topping it with the sautéed shrimp and garnishing with chopped fresh basil leaves.

12- Enjoy your Shrimp and Grilled Zucchini Risotto!

Nutritional Information (per serving):

Calories: Approximately 500-600
Protein: 25-30g
Fat: 10-15g
Carbohydrates: 70-75g
Fiber: 5-7g
Sugars: 5-7g

Glycemic Index (GI): The GI of risotto primarily depends on the Arborio rice and is moderate. The presence of shrimp and zucchini may influence the overall glycemic response. Individual responses may vary, so consult a healthcare professional for personalized dietary advice.

Salmon Fettuccine with Lemon Cream Sauce

- Difficulty Level: ☐☐☐
- Preparation Time: 15 minutes
- Cooking Time: 20 minutes
- Cooking Skill: Intermediate

Ingredients for Two:

- 8 oz (about 225g) fettuccine pasta

- 2 salmon fillets (about 6 oz each), skinless
- 1 tablespoon olive oil
- Salt and black pepper, to taste
- 2 cloves garlic, minced
- 1 cup heavy cream
- Zest of 1 lemon
- Juice of 1 lemon
- 1/2 cup grated Parmesan cheese
- 2 tablespoons fresh dill, chopped (for garnish)
- Lemon slices (for garnish)

Instructions:

1- Cook the fettuccine pasta according to the package instructions until al dente. Drain and set aside.

2- Season the salmon fillets with salt and black pepper to taste. In a large skillet, heat the olive oil over medium-high heat. Add the salmon fillets and cook for about 4-5 minutes per side until they are cooked through and flake easily. Remove the salmon from the skillet and set aside.

3- In the same skillet, add the minced garlic and cook for about 1 minute until fragrant.

4- Pour in the heavy cream and bring it to a simmer. Let it simmer for about 2-3 minutes, stirring occasionally.

5- Stir in the lemon zest, lemon juice, and grated Parmesan cheese. Continue to cook for another 2-3 minutes, allowing the sauce to thicken.

6- Break the cooked salmon into bite-sized pieces and add it to the sauce. Cook for

an additional 2 minutes, stirring gently to combine.

7- Toss the cooked fettuccine in the lemon cream sauce, ensuring the pasta is well coated.

8- Serve the Salmon Fettuccine with a sprinkle of fresh dill and lemon slices for garnish.

9- Enjoy your Salmon Fettuccine with Lemon Cream Sauce!

Nutritional Information (per serving):

Calories: Approximately 600-700
Protein: 30-35g
Fat: 40-45g
Carbohydrates: 35-40g
Fiber: 2-4g
Sugars: 2-3g

Glycemic Index (GI): Fettuccine pasta is a carbohydrate-rich component of this dish, so the overall GI may be moderate. The presence of protein from the salmon and the fat content can also influence the glycemic response. Individual responses may vary, so consult a healthcare professional for personalized dietary advice.

Sea Cucumber Spaghetti with Cherry Tomatoes and Basil

- Difficulty Level: ☐☐
- Preparation Time: 20 minutes
- Cooking Time: 10 minutes
- Cooking Skill: Intermediate

Ingredients for Two:

- 8 oz sea cucumber spaghetti (or substitute regular spaghetti)
- 1 cup cherry tomatoes, halved
- 1/4 cup fresh basil leaves, chopped
- 2 cloves garlic, minced
- 1/4 cup extra-virgin olive oil
- Salt and black pepper, to taste
- Grated Parmesan cheese (optional, for garnish)

Instructions:

1- Cook the sea cucumber spaghetti (or regular spaghetti) according to the package instructions until al dente. Drain and set aside.

2- In a large skillet, heat the extra-virgin olive oil over medium heat. Add the minced garlic and cook for about 1 minute until fragrant.

3- Add the cherry tomatoes to the skillet and sauté for 3-4 minutes until they begin to soften.

4- Stir in the fresh basil leaves and cook for an additional 1-2 minutes, allowing the flavors to combine.

5- Toss the cooked sea cucumber spaghetti (or regular spaghetti) into the skillet with the tomato and basil mixture. Season with salt and black pepper to taste.

6- Gently mix everything together, ensuring the pasta is well coated with the tomato and basil sauce.

7- Serve your Sea Cucumber Spaghetti with Cherry Tomatoes and Basil hot, garnished with grated Parmesan cheese if desired.

8- Enjoy your Sea Cucumber Spaghetti with a unique twist!

Nutritional Information (per serving):

Calories: Approximately 350-400

Protein: 7-9g

Fat: 15-18g

Carbohydrates: 50-55g

Fiber: 4-6g

Sugars: 4-6g

Glycemic Index (GI): Pasta typically has a moderate GI, but sea cucumber spaghetti may have a different glycemic response. Individual responses can vary, so consult a healthcare professional for personalized dietary advice.

Buckwheat Tagliatelle with Smoked Salmon and Arugula

- Difficulty Level: ☐☐
- Preparation Time: 15 minutes
- Cooking Time: 10 minutes
- Cooking Skill: Intermediate

Ingredients for Two:

- 8 oz buckwheat tagliatelle
- 4 oz smoked salmon, thinly sliced
- 2 cups fresh arugula
- 1/4 cup crème fraîche
- 2 tablespoons fresh dill, chopped
- 1 lemon, zested and juiced
- Salt and black pepper, to taste

Instructions:

1- Cook the buckwheat tagliatelle according to the package instructions until al dente. Drain and set aside.

2 In a large bowl, combine the crème fraîche, lemon zest, and lemon juice. Mix until well combined.

3- Toss the cooked and drained buckwheat tagliatelle into the bowl with the crème fraîche mixture. Gently stir to coat the pasta evenly.

4- Add the smoked salmon slices and fresh dill to the bowl. Mix gently to combine.

5- Add the fresh arugula to the pasta mixture and gently toss until the arugula starts to wilt slightly.

6- Season with salt and black pepper to taste.

7- Serve your Buckwheat Tagliatelle with Smoked Salmon and Arugula immediately, garnished with extra dill if desired.

8- Enjoy the delightful combination of flavors!

Nutritional Information (per serving):

Calories: Approximately 450-500

Protein: 20-25g

Fat: 20-25g

Carbohydrates: 50-60g

Fiber: 6-8g

Sugars: 2-3g

Glycemic Index (GI): Buckwheat pasta generally has a lower GI compared to traditional wheat pasta, resulting in a slower and more controlled increase in blood sugar levels. However, individual responses can vary, so consult a healthcare professional for personalized dietary advice.

MEAT DISHES

Veal Scaloppine with Marsala Wine and Mushrooms

- Difficulty Level: ☐☐☐
- Preparation Time: 15 minutes
- Cooking Time: 20 minutes
- Cooking Skill: Intermediate

Ingredients for Two:

- 4 veal scaloppine (thinly sliced veal cutlets)
- 1/2 cup all-purpose flour
- Salt and black pepper, to taste
- 2 tablespoons olive oil
- 1/2 cup Marsala wine
- 1/2 cup chicken or vegetable broth
- 8 oz cremini or white mushrooms, sliced
- 2 cloves garlic, minced
- 2 tablespoons fresh parsley, chopped
- 2 tablespoons unsalted butter

Instructions:

1- Season the veal scaloppine with salt and black pepper. Dredge them in flour, shaking off any excess.

2- In a large skillet, heat the olive oil over medium-high heat. Add the veal scaloppine and cook for about 2-3 minutes per side until they're browned and cooked through. Remove the veal from the skillet and set aside.

3- In the same skillet, add the mushrooms and minced garlic. Sauté for about 5 minutes or until the mushrooms are tender and any liquid has evaporated.

4- Pour in the Marsala wine and chicken or vegetable broth. Stir to combine and scrape up any browned bits from the bottom of the skillet. Simmer for about 5-7 minutes or until the sauce has reduced by half and thickened.

5- Return the cooked veal scaloppine to the skillet and simmer for another 2-3 minutes to heat them through.

6- Stir in the chopped fresh parsley and unsalted butter, allowing the butter to melt and the sauce to become creamy.

7- Taste the sauce and adjust the seasoning with more salt and black pepper if needed.

8- Serve your Veal Scaloppine with Marsala Wine and Mushrooms hot, garnished with extra parsley if desired.

9- Enjoy this classic Italian dish with your choice of side, such as mashed potatoes or pasta!

Nutritional Information (per serving):

Calories: Approximately 450-500

Protein: 35-40g

Fat: 18-20g

Carbohydrates: 30-35g

Fiber: 2-3g

Sugars: 3-4g

Glycemic Index (GI): This dish contains little to no high-GI ingredients, so it should have a low to moderate impact on blood sugar levels. However, the specific GI can vary based on portion size and the ingredients used. For personalized dietary advice, consult a healthcare professional.

Roast Turkey with Sweet Potatoes and Green Beans

- Difficulty Level: ☐☐
- Preparation Time: 20 minutes
- Cooking Time: 2 hours
- Cooking Skill: Intermediate

Ingredients for Two:

- 2 turkey drumsticks or breast portions
- 2 large sweet potatoes, peeled and cut into chunks
- 1 cup green beans, trimmed
- 2 tablespoons olive oil
- 2 cloves garlic, minced
- 1 teaspoon dried thyme
- 1 teaspoon dried rosemary
- Salt and black pepper, to taste
- 1/2 cup chicken or vegetable broth
- 2 tablespoons fresh parsley, chopped

Instructions:

1- Preheat your oven to 350°F (175°C).

2- In a large ovenproof dish, arrange the turkey drumsticks or breast portions.

3- In a separate bowl, combine the olive oil, minced garlic, dried thyme, dried rosemary, salt, and black pepper. Mix well.

4- Brush the turkey with the olive oil and herb mixture, making sure it's evenly coated.

5- Place the sweet potato chunks and green beans around the turkey in the ovenproof dish.

6- Pour the chicken or vegetable broth over the vegetables.

7- Cover the dish with aluminum foil and place it in the preheated oven.

8- Roast for approximately 1.5 to 2 hours, or until the turkey is cooked through (the internal temperature should reach 165°F or 74°C).

9- Remove the foil for the last 15-20 minutes of cooking to allow the turkey and vegetables to brown.

10- Check that the sweet potatoes and green beans are tender.

11- Garnish with fresh chopped parsley before serving.

12- Serve your Roast Turkey with Sweet Potatoes and Green Beans hot, and enjoy!

Nutritional Information (per serving):

Calories: Approximately 400-450
Protein: 30-35g
Fat: 12-15g
Carbohydrates: 40-45g
Fiber: 7-8g
Sugars: 10-12g

Glycemic Index (GI): This dish has a low to moderate GI, primarily from the sweet potatoes and green beans. The specific GI can vary based on portion size and the ingredients used. If you have specific dietary concerns, consult a healthcare professional for advice.

Beef Steak with Steamed Broccoli

- Difficulty Level: ☐ ☐
- Preparation Time: 15 minutes
- Cooking Time: 10-15 minutes
- Cooking Skill: Intermediate

Ingredients for Two:

- 2 beef steaks (sirloin, ribeye, or your preferred cut)
- 2 cups broccoli florets
- 2 tablespoons olive oil
- 2 cloves garlic, minced
- Salt and black pepper, to taste
- 1 tablespoon fresh lemon juice (optional)
- Fresh parsley, for garnish (optional)

Instructions:

1- Season the beef steaks with salt and black pepper on both sides. Let them sit at room temperature for about 15 minutes.

2- While the steaks rest, prepare your steamer for the broccoli.

3- Steam the broccoli florets for about 5-7 minutes, or until they are tender-crisp. You want them to retain a bit of crunch. Set aside.

4- In a skillet, heat the olive oil over medium-high heat.

5- Once the oil is hot, add the minced garlic and sauté for about 30 seconds until fragrant, but be careful not to let it brown.

6- Add the seasoned steaks to the hot skillet.

7- For medium-rare steaks, cook them for about 3-4 minutes per side. Adjust the cooking time based on your desired level of doneness.

8- Transfer the steaks to a plate and let them rest for a few minutes before slicing.

9- While the steaks rest, drizzle fresh lemon juice over the broccoli (if using).

10- Slice the steaks into thin strips.

11- Serve the sliced beef alongside the steamed broccoli.

12- Garnish with fresh parsley if desired.

13- Enjoy your Beef Steak with Steamed Broccoli!

Nutritional Information (per serving):

Calories: Approximately 400-450
Protein: 35-40g
Fat: 25-30g
Carbohydrates: 6-10g
Fiber: 2-4g
Sugars: 2-3g

Glycemic Index (GI): This dish is low in carbohydrates, so the glycemic index is minimal. It primarily comes from the trace carbohydrates in the broccoli.

Lean Meatballs with Tomato Sauce and Zucchini

- Difficulty Level: ☐☐
- Preparation Time: 30 minutes
- Cooking Time: 30 minutes
- Cooking Skill: Intermediate

Ingredients for Two:

For the Lean Meatballs:

- 1/2 pound lean ground beef or turkey
- 1/4 cup breadcrumbs
- 1/4 cup grated Parmesan cheese
- 1/4 cup finely chopped onion
- 1 clove garlic, minced
- 1 egg
- 1 tablespoon fresh parsley, chopped
- Salt and black pepper, to taste

For the Tomato Sauce:

- 1 cup crushed tomatoes

- *1/2 teaspoon dried basil*
- *1/2 teaspoon dried oregano*
- *Salt and black pepper, to taste*

For the Zucchini:

- *2 medium zucchinis, spiralized or thinly sliced*
- *1 tablespoon olive oil*
- *1 clove garlic, minced*
- *Salt and black pepper, to taste*

Instructions:

1- *Preheat your oven to 375°F (190°C).*

2- *In a large mixing bowl, combine the lean ground beef or turkey, breadcrumbs, grated Parmesan cheese, chopped onion, minced garlic, egg, chopped parsley, salt, and black pepper. Mix until well combined.*

3- *Shape the mixture into meatballs. You should get around 10-12 meatballs.*

4- *Place the meatballs on a baking sheet lined with parchment paper. Bake in the preheated oven for 20-25 minutes or until cooked through.*

5- *While the meatballs are baking, prepare the tomato sauce. In a saucepan, combine the crushed tomatoes, dried basil, dried oregano, salt, and black pepper. Simmer over low heat for about 10-15 minutes.*

6- *In a separate pan, heat the olive oil over medium heat. Add the minced garlic and sauté for about 30 seconds. Add the zucchini noodles and sauté for 3-5*

minutes or until they soften but still have a bit of crunch. Season with salt and black pepper.

7- *Once the meatballs are cooked, serve them over the zucchini noodles and drizzle the tomato sauce on top.*

8- *Garnish with additional chopped parsley if desired.*

9- *Enjoy your Lean Meatballs with Tomato Sauce and Zucchini!*

Nutritional Information (per serving):

Calories: Approximately 350-400

Protein: 30-35g

Fat: 15-20g

Carbohydrates: 20-25g

Fiber: 5-8g

Sugars: 8-10g

Glycemic Index (GI): This dish has a low to moderate glycemic index, mainly coming from the zucchini and tomato sauce.

Pork with Black Pepper, Cabbage, and Carrots

- *Difficulty Level:* ☐☐
- *Preparation Time: 20 minutes*
- *Cooking Time: 20 minutes*
- *Cooking Skill: Intermediate*

Ingredients for Two:

For the Pork:

- *2 boneless pork chops or pork tenderloin medallions*
- *2 tablespoons black peppercorns, crushed*
- *1 tablespoon olive oil*
- *Salt, to taste*

For the Vegetables:

- *2 cups cabbage, thinly sliced*
- *1 cup carrots, julienned*
- *2 cloves garlic, minced*
- *1 tablespoon olive oil*
- *Salt, to taste*

Instructions:

1- *Place the black peppercorns on a plate. Press both sides of the pork chops or tenderloin medallions into the crushed peppercorns to coat them thoroughly. Season with a pinch of salt.*

2- *In a large skillet, heat 1 tablespoon of olive oil over medium-high heat. Add the pork and cook for about 4-5 minutes on each side, or until the internal temperature reaches 145°F (63°C) for pork chops or 160°F (71°C) for pork tenderloin medallions. Remove the pork from the skillet and let it rest for a few minutes.*

3- *In the same skillet, add another tablespoon of olive oil. Add the minced garlic and sauté for about 30 seconds or until fragrant.*

4- *Add the sliced cabbage and julienned carrots to the skillet. Sauté for 5-7*

minutes, or until the vegetables are tender but still slightly crisp. Season with salt to taste.

5- *Slice the rested pork into thin medallions.*

6- *Serve the sliced pork on a plate alongside the sautéed cabbage and carrots. Garnish with additional crushed black pepper if desired.*

7- *Enjoy your Pork with Black Pepper, Cabbage, and Carrots!*

Nutritional Information (per serving):

Calories: Approximately 300-350

Protein: 25-30g

Fat: 15-18g

Carbohydrates: 15-20g

Fiber: 4-6g

Sugars: 6-8g

Glycemic Index (GI): This dish has a low glycemic index due to the absence of high-carb ingredients.

Lemon and Rosemary Chicken with Orzo

- *Difficulty Level: ☐☐*
- *Preparation Time: 15 minutes*
- *Cooking Time: 25 minutes*
- *Cooking Skill: Intermediate*

Ingredients for Two:

For the Chicken:

- *2 boneless, skinless chicken breasts*
- *2 tablespoons olive oil*
- *2 cloves garlic, minced*
- *1 lemon, juiced and zested*
- *2 sprigs fresh rosemary*
- *Salt and pepper, to taste*

For the Orzo:

- *1 cup orzo pasta*
- *2 cups chicken or vegetable broth*
- *1/2 cup frozen peas*
- *1/4 cup grated Parmesan cheese*
- *Salt and pepper, to taste*

Instructions:

For the Chicken:

1- *Preheat your oven to 375°F (190°C).*

2- *Season the chicken breasts with salt and pepper.*

3- *In an oven-safe skillet, heat 2 tablespoons of olive oil over medium-high heat. Add the chicken breasts and sear for 2-3 minutes on each side until they're golden brown.*

4- *Remove the chicken from the skillet and set it aside. In the same skillet, add minced garlic and sauté for about 30 seconds, or until fragrant.*

5- *Return the chicken to the skillet, add the juice and zest of one lemon, and tuck the rosemary sprigs alongside the chicken.*

6- *Transfer the skillet to the preheated oven and roast for 15-20 minutes or until the chicken reaches an internal temperature of 165°F (74°C). Remove from the oven and let it rest for a few minutes.*

For the Orzo:

1- *In a separate pot, bring 2 cups of chicken or vegetable broth to a boil.*

2- *Add 1 cup of orzo and cook according to the package instructions until al dente, usually about 8-10 minutes.*

3- *In the last minute of cooking, add 1/2 cup of frozen peas to the orzo and let them cook together.*

4- *Drain any excess liquid from the orzo and peas, and then stir in 1/4 cup of grated Parmesan cheese. Season with salt and pepper to taste.*

To Serve:

1- *Divide the lemon and rosemary chicken into two servings and place it on a plate alongside the orzo and peas mixture.*

2- *Enjoy your Lemon and Rosemary Chicken with Orzo!*

Nutritional Information (per serving):

Calories: Approximately 400-450

Protein: 30-35g

Fat: 15-20g

Carbohydrates: 30-35g

Fiber: 3-4g

Sugars: 2-3g

Glycemic Index (GI): Orzo typically has a moderate GI, while chicken, vegetables, and cheese have a low GI, making this dish a balanced meal.

Chicken Teriyaki with Grilled Vegetables

- Difficulty Level: ☐☐
- Preparation Time: 15 minutes
- Marinating Time: 30 minutes
- Cooking Time: 15 minutes
- Cooking Skill: Intermediate

Ingredients for Two:

For the Chicken:

- 2 boneless, skinless chicken breasts
- 1/2 cup teriyaki sauce
- 2 cloves garlic, minced
- 1 tablespoon grated fresh ginger
- 2 tablespoons vegetable oil
- Salt and pepper, to taste

For the Grilled Vegetables:

- 2 bell peppers (assorted colors), sliced
- 1 zucchini, sliced
- 1 red onion, cut into wedges
- 1 cup cherry tomatoes
- 2 tablespoons vegetable oil
- Salt and pepper, to taste

Instructions:

For the Chicken:

1- In a bowl, combine 1/2 cup of teriyaki sauce, minced garlic, grated fresh ginger, 2 tablespoons of vegetable oil, and a pinch of salt and pepper.

2- Place the chicken breasts in a resealable plastic bag or a shallow dish. Pour the teriyaki marinade over the chicken, ensuring it's well coated. Seal the bag or cover the dish and refrigerate for at least 30 minutes to marinate.

3- Preheat your grill or grill pan over medium-high heat.

4- Remove the chicken from the marinade, allowing any excess to drip off, and grill for approximately 6-7 minutes per side or until fully cooked (the internal temperature should reach 165°F or 74°C). Baste with additional marinade while grilling.

5- Once cooked, remove the chicken from the grill, tent with aluminum foil, and let it rest for a few minutes.

For the Grilled Vegetables:

1- While the chicken is marinating, toss the sliced bell peppers, zucchini, red onion, and cherry tomatoes in 2 tablespoons of vegetable oil. Season with salt and pepper.

2- Preheat your grill or grill pan over medium-high heat. Grill the vegetables for about 3-5 minutes per side or until they have grill marks and are tender.

To Serve:

1- Divide the grilled chicken and vegetables between two plates, drizzle any remaining teriyaki sauce over the chicken, and serve.

2- Enjoy your Chicken Teriyaki with Grilled Vegetables!

Nutritional Information (per serving):

Calories: Approximately 350-400

Protein: 30-35g

Fat: 15-20g

Carbohydrates: 25-30g

Fiber: 5-6g

Sugars: 15-20g

Glycemic Index (GI): Teriyaki sauce typically contains sugars, so this dish may have a moderate to high GI due to the sugars. The vegetables contribute fiber, which can help moderate the overall GI.

Beef Fajitas with Bell Peppers and Onions

- Difficulty Level: ☐☐
- Preparation Time: 15 minutes
- Marinating Time: 30 minutes
- Cooking Time: 15 minutes
- Cooking Skill: Intermediate

Ingredients for Two:

For the Marinade:

- 1/4 cup lime juice
- 1/4 cup vegetable oil
- 2 cloves garlic, minced
- 1 teaspoon ground cumin
- 1 teaspoon chili powder

- 1/2 teaspoon paprika
- Salt and pepper, to taste

For the Fajitas:

- 2 boneless beef steaks (skirt steak or flank steak work well)
- 1 red bell pepper, sliced
- 1 green bell pepper, sliced
- 1 yellow onion, sliced
- 8 small flour tortillas
- Sour cream, guacamole, and salsa for serving

Instructions:

For the Marinade:

1- In a bowl, whisk together lime juice, vegetable oil, minced garlic, ground cumin, chili powder, paprika, salt, and pepper to create the marinade.

For the Fajitas:

2- Place the beef steaks in a resealable plastic bag or a shallow dish. Pour the marinade over the steaks, ensuring they are well coated. Seal the bag or cover the dish and refrigerate for at least 30 minutes to marinate.

Preheat your grill or grill pan over medium-high heat.

3- Remove the beef from the marinade and grill for approximately 3-4 minutes per side for medium-rare or longer for your desired level of doneness. Once done, transfer the beef to a cutting board and let it rest for a few minutes.

4- While the beef is resting, grill the sliced bell peppers and onions until they're slightly charred and tender, about 5-7 minutes.

5- Slice the rested beef against the grain into thin strips.

6- Warm the flour tortillas on the grill for about 30 seconds per side.

7- To serve, fill each tortilla with beef strips, grilled bell peppers, and onions. Add your favorite toppings like sour cream, guacamole, and salsa.

8- Enjoy your Beef Fajitas with Bell Peppers and Onions!

Nutritional Information (per serving, excluding toppings):

Calories: Approximately 400-450

Protein: 30-35g

Fat: 20-25g

Carbohydrates: 25-30g

Fiber: 4-5g

Sugars: 4-5g

Glycemic Index (GI): The GI for this meal is moderate. The tortillas may contribute to the GI, but the presence of protein, fiber, and vegetables helps to moderate the overall impact on blood sugar.

Chicken Curry with Coconut Milk and Spinach

- Difficulty Level: ☐☐
- Preparation Time: 15 minutes
- Cooking Time: 25 minutes
- Cooking Skill: Intermediate

Ingredients for Two:

- 2 boneless, skinless chicken breasts, cut into bite-sized pieces
- 1 onion, finely chopped
- 2 cloves garlic, minced
- 1 tablespoon fresh ginger, minced
- 2 tablespoons curry paste (red, green, or yellow, depending on your preference)
- 1 can (14 oz) coconut milk
- 2 cups fresh spinach leaves
- 1 tablespoon vegetable oil
- Salt and pepper, to taste
- Cooked rice, for serving

Instructions:

1- In a large skillet, heat the vegetable oil over medium-high heat. Add the chopped onion and cook until it becomes translucent.

2- Add the minced garlic and ginger to the skillet and cook for another minute until fragrant.

3- Stir in the curry paste and cook for 1-2 minutes, stirring constantly.

4- Add the bite-sized chicken pieces to the skillet and cook until they are no longer pink on the outside.

5- Pour in the can of coconut milk and season with salt and pepper. Stir well and let the mixture come to a gentle simmer.

6- Reduce the heat to low, cover the skillet, and let the curry simmer for about 15-20 minutes, allowing the chicken to cook through and the flavors to meld.

7- Just before serving, stir in the fresh spinach leaves. Cook for an additional 1-2 minutes until the spinach wilts and becomes tender.

8- Taste and adjust the seasoning if needed.

9- Serve your chicken curry with coconut milk and spinach over cooked rice.

10- Enjoy your Chicken Curry with Coconut Milk and Spinach!

Nutritional Information (per serving, without rice):

Calories: Approximately 350-400

Protein: 25-30g

Fat: 20-25g

Carbohydrates: 10-15g

Fiber: 2-3g

Sugars: 2-3g

Glycemic Index (GI): The GI for this meal is moderate to low, depending on the amount of rice consumed. The curry itself is relatively low GI, while the rice may have a higher GI, depending on the variety and preparation.

Roast Chicken with Mashed Sweet Potatoes and Steamed Broccoli

- Difficulty Level: ☐☐
- Preparation Time: 20 minutes
- Cooking Time: 1 hour

- Cooking Skill: Intermediate

Ingredients for Two:

For Roast Chicken:

- 2 bone-in, skin-on chicken breasts
- 2 tablespoons olive oil
- 1 teaspoon dried thyme
- 1 teaspoon dried rosemary
- Salt and pepper, to taste

For Mashed Sweet Potatoes:

- 2 medium sweet potatoes, peeled and cut into chunks
- 2 tablespoons unsalted butter
- 2-3 tablespoons milk (as needed)
- Salt and pepper, to taste

For Steamed Broccoli:

- 2 cups fresh broccoli florets
- Water for steaming
- Salt, to taste

Instructions:

Roast Chicken:

1- Preheat your oven to 375°F (190°C).
2- Rub the chicken breasts with olive oil and season them with dried thyme, rosemary, salt, and pepper.
3- Place the chicken breasts on a baking sheet or in an oven-safe dish.
4- Roast the chicken in the preheated oven for approximately 45-60 minutes, or until the internal temperature reaches 165°F (74°C) and the skin is golden and crispy.

5- Once done, remove the chicken from the oven and let it rest for a few minutes before serving.

Mashed Sweet Potatoes:

6- Place the sweet potato chunks in a pot of boiling water. Cook until they are tender, which should take about 15-20 minutes.
7- Drain the sweet potatoes and transfer them to a bowl.
8- Mash the sweet potatoes with a potato masher or fork.
9- Add the butter and milk, and continue mashing until the mixture reaches your desired consistency. Season with salt and pepper to taste.

Steamed Broccoli:

10- Place the fresh broccoli florets in a steaming basket or a microwave-safe dish.
11- Add a small amount of water to the bottom of the pot or dish, and cover with a lid or microwave-safe plate.
12- Steam the broccoli for about 4-5 minutes until it's tender yet still crisp.
13- Season with a pinch of salt.

14- Serve your Roast Chicken with Mashed Sweet Potatoes and Steamed Broccoli. Enjoy!

Nutritional Information (per serving):

Calories: Approximately 450-500 (may vary based on portion sizes)

Protein: 30-35g

Fat: 20-25g

Carbohydrates: 30-35g

Fiber: 5-7g

Sugars: 7-10g

Glycemic Index (GI): The GI of this meal is moderate, with sweet potatoes being the main carbohydrate source and having a lower GI than regular white potatoes. The broccoli has a low GI, which helps balance the overall meal's GI.

SEAFOOD DISHES

Baked Salmon with Walnut Crust and Spinach

- Difficulty Level: ☐☐
- Preparation Time: 15 minutes
- Cooking Time: 15 minutes
- Cooking Skill: Intermediate

Ingredients for Two:

For the Walnut-Crusted Salmon:

- 2 salmon fillets (6-8 ounces each)
- 1/2 cup chopped walnuts
- 1/4 cup whole wheat breadcrumbs
- 1 tablespoon Dijon mustard
- 1 tablespoon honey
- 1 tablespoon olive oil
- Salt and pepper, to taste

For the Sautéed Spinach:

- 4 cups fresh spinach leaves
- 2 cloves garlic, minced
- 1 tablespoon olive oil
- Salt and pepper, to taste

Instructions:

Walnut-Crusted Salmon:

1- *Preheat your oven to 375°F (190°C).*
2- *In a bowl, combine the chopped walnuts, whole wheat breadcrumbs, Dijon mustard, honey, and olive oil. Mix until you have a thick paste.*
3- *Season the salmon fillets with salt and pepper.*
4- *Place the salmon fillets on a baking sheet lined with parchment paper.*
5- *Spread the walnut mixture evenly over the top of each salmon fillet, pressing it down gently to adhere.*
6- *Bake the salmon in the preheated oven for about 12-15 minutes or until the salmon flakes easily with a fork and the crust is golden.*

Sautéed Spinach:

7- *In a large skillet, heat olive oil over medium heat.*
8- *Add minced garlic and sauté for about 30 seconds until fragrant.*
9- *Add the fresh spinach leaves and cook, stirring occasionally, for 2-3 minutes until the spinach wilts.*
10- *Season with salt and pepper to taste.*

11- *Serve your Walnut-Crusted Salmon with a side of Sautéed Spinach. Enjoy!*

Nutritional Information (per serving):

Calories: Approximately 400-450 (may vary based on portion sizes)

Protein: 35-40g

Fat: 20-25g

Carbohydrates: 20-25g

Fiber: 4-6g

Sugars: 6-8g

Glycemic Index (GI): This meal has a low to moderate GI due to the minimal carbohydrate content from breadcrumbs and honey. The salmon and spinach have negligible effects on blood sugar levels.

Grilled Shrimp with Citrus Sauce

- *Difficulty Level:* ☐☐
- *Preparation Time: 15 minutes*
- *Cooking Time: 5 minutes*
- *Cooking Skill: Easy*

Ingredients for Two:

For the Grilled Shrimp:

- *12 large shrimp, peeled and deveined*
- *1 tablespoon olive oil*
- *1 clove garlic, minced*
- *1 teaspoon paprika*
- *Salt and pepper, to taste*
- *Lemon wedges, for serving*

For the Citrus Sauce:

- *1/4 cup fresh orange juice*
- *2 tablespoons fresh lemon juice*
- *1 tablespoon fresh lime juice*
- *1 tablespoon honey or maple syrup*
- *1/2 teaspoon grated orange zest*
- *1/2 teaspoon grated lemon zest*
- *1/2 teaspoon grated lime zest*
- *1/4 teaspoon red pepper flakes (adjust to taste)*
- *Salt and pepper, to taste*

Instructions:

Grilled Shrimp:

1- In a bowl, combine olive oil, minced garlic, paprika, salt, and pepper.
2- Add the peeled and deveined shrimp to the bowl and toss to coat them with the marinade.
3- Preheat your grill to medium-high heat.
4- Thread the marinated shrimp onto skewers.
5- Grill the shrimp for about 2-3 minutes on each side or until they turn pink and opaque.

Citrus Sauce:

6- In a small saucepan, combine the fresh orange juice, lemon juice, lime juice, honey (or maple syrup), orange zest, lemon zest, lime zest, and red pepper flakes.
7- Bring the mixture to a gentle simmer and cook for 2-3 minutes, allowing it to thicken slightly.
8- Season the sauce with salt and pepper to taste.

9- Serve the grilled shrimp with the citrus sauce on the side. Garnish with lemon wedges. Enjoy!

Nutritional Information (per serving):

Calories: Approximately 180-220 (may vary based on portion sizes)
Protein: 15-20g
Fat: 7-10g
Carbohydrates: 15-20g
Fiber: 1-2g
Sugars: 12-15g

Glycemic Index (GI): The glycemic index for this meal is low, primarily due to the absence of high-carbohydrate ingredients. The citrus sauce may have a moderate impact on blood sugar levels due to its natural sugar content.

Sicilian Swordfish with Cherry Tomatoes and Olives

- Difficulty Level: ☐☐
- Preparation Time: 15 minutes
- Cooking Time: 20 minutes
- Cooking Skill: Intermediate

Ingredients for Two:

- 2 swordfish steaks (about 6-8 ounces each)
- 1 cup cherry tomatoes, halved
- 1/4 cup pitted green olives
- 1/4 cup pitted black olives
- 2 cloves garlic, minced
- 2 tablespoons capers
- 2 tablespoons fresh basil, chopped
- 2 tablespoons fresh parsley, chopped
- 2 tablespoons olive oil
- Salt and pepper, to taste
- Red pepper flakes (optional, for some heat)

Instructions:

1- Start by seasoning the swordfish steaks with salt, pepper, and a drizzle of olive oil.

2- Heat a large skillet over medium-high heat and add a bit of olive oil. Once hot, add the swordfish steaks.

3- Cook the swordfish for about 4-5 minutes per side, or until it's cooked through and has a nice sear. Once done, remove the swordfish from the skillet and set it aside.

4- In the same skillet, add more olive oil if needed. Add the minced garlic and cook for about a minute until fragrant.

5- Add the halved cherry tomatoes and cook for another 4-5 minutes until they start to soften.

6- Stir in the green and black olives, capers, and red pepper flakes (if you want some heat). Cook for an additional 3-4 minutes.

7- Return the cooked swordfish steaks to the skillet and heat them through, about 2-3 minutes.

8- Stir in the fresh basil and parsley.

9- Taste and adjust the seasoning with salt and pepper, if necessary.

10- Serve the swordfish steaks with the tomato, olive, and caper sauce on top.

11- Enjoy your Sicilian-style swordfish with a side of your choice, such as steamed vegetables or a simple salad!

Nutritional Information (per serving):

Calories: Approximately 350-400 (may vary based on portion sizes)

Protein: 30-35g

Fat: 20-25g

Carbohydrates: 10-15g

Fiber: 3-4g

Sugars: 4-6g

Glycemic Index (GI): This meal has a low glycemic index due to the presence of mainly low-carb ingredients such as swordfish, olives, and fresh herbs. The cherry tomatoes may slightly increase the GI, but the overall impact on blood sugar should still be moderate.

Grilled Octopus with Potatoes and Cherry Tomatoes

- Difficulty Level: □□□
- Preparation Time: 20 minutes
- Cooking Time: 1 hour
- Cooking Skill: Intermediate

Ingredients for Two:

- 1 whole octopus (about 1 kg or 2.2 pounds), cleaned
- 500g (about 1.1 pounds) small potatoes, halved
- 1 cup cherry tomatoes
- 3 cloves garlic, minced
- 1/4 cup fresh parsley, chopped
- Zest and juice of 1 lemon
- 1/4 cup extra virgin olive oil
- Salt and black pepper, to taste
- Red pepper flakes (optional, for some heat)

Instructions:

1- Start by cooking the octopus. In a large pot of boiling water, immerse the octopus three times briefly (about 5 seconds each time). This helps to tenderize the octopus. After that, add the octopus to the boiling water and simmer for about 45 minutes to 1 hour until tender. You can check for doneness by *inserting a knife; it should slide in easily. Once done, remove from the water and let it cool.*

2- *While the octopus is cooling, preheat your grill to medium-high heat.*

3- *In a large bowl, combine the halved potatoes, cherry tomatoes, minced garlic, and fresh parsley. Drizzle with olive oil and season with salt, black pepper, and red pepper flakes if you like it spicy. Toss well to coat.*

4- *Once the octopus has cooled, cut it into large pieces.*

5- *Thread the octopus pieces onto skewers, and place the potato and tomato mixture in a grill basket or on a grill-safe tray.*

6- *Grill the octopus for about 4-5 minutes per side until it has grill marks and is heated through.*

7- *Grill the potatoes and cherry tomatoes in the grill basket for about 15-20 minutes, turning occasionally until they're tender and slightly charred.*

8- *While still hot from the grill, drizzle the zest and juice of one lemon over the grilled octopus, potatoes, and cherry tomatoes.*

9- *Serve the grilled octopus alongside the potatoes and cherry tomatoes. Garnish with extra fresh parsley, if desired.*

10- *Enjoy your grilled octopus with a Mediterranean flair!*

Nutritional Information (per serving):

Calories: Approximately 350-400 (may vary based on portion sizes)

Protein: 25-30g

Fat: 15-20g

Carbohydrates: 30-35g

Fiber: 5-7g

Sugars: 4-6g

Glycemic Index (GI): This meal has a low glycemic index due to the presence of octopus, potatoes, and cherry tomatoes. The carbohydrates from the potatoes and tomatoes are relatively slow to digest, making it a balanced and satisfying meal.

Fish Skewers with Zucchini and Cherry Tomatoes

- *Difficulty Level:* ☐☐
- *Preparation Time: 30 minutes*
- *Cooking Time: 10 minutes*
- *Cooking Skill: Intermediate*

Ingredients for Two:

For the Fish Skewers:

- *300g (10.5 oz) white fish fillets (such as cod or tilapia), cut into chunks*
- *1 lemon, zested and juiced*
- *2 cloves garlic, minced*
- *2 tablespoons olive oil*
- *Salt and black pepper, to taste*
- *Wooden skewers, soaked in water for 30 minutes*

For the Zucchini and Cherry Tomatoes:

- *2 small zucchinis, sliced into rounds*
- *1 cup cherry tomatoes*
- *2 tablespoons olive oil*
- *Salt and black pepper, to taste*
- *Fresh basil leaves, for garnish*

Instructions:

1- *In a bowl, combine the lemon zest, lemon juice, minced garlic, olive oil, salt, and black pepper. Add the fish chunks and toss to coat. Let it marinate for about 15 minutes.*

2- *Thread the marinated fish chunks onto the soaked wooden skewers, alternating with pieces of zucchini and cherry tomatoes.*

3- *Preheat your grill to medium-high heat.*

4- *In a separate bowl, toss the zucchini rounds and cherry tomatoes with olive oil, salt, and black pepper.*

5- *Grill the fish skewers for about 3-4 minutes per side, or until the fish is cooked through and has grill marks.*

6- *At the same time, grill the zucchini and cherry tomatoes for about 2-3 minutes per side, or until they are tender and slightly charred.*

7- *Once everything is grilled and cooked to your liking, remove from the grill.*

8- *Arrange the grilled fish skewers on a platter, alongside the zucchini and cherry tomatoes.*

9- *Garnish with fresh basil leaves, and drizzle any remaining lemon marinade over the skewers and veggies.*

10- *Serve hot and enjoy your delicious fish skewers with zucchini and cherry tomatoes!*

Nutritional Information (per serving):

Calories: Approximately 350-400 (may vary based on portion sizes)

Protein: 25-30g

Fat: 20-25g

Carbohydrates: 10-15g

Fiber: 3-4g

Sugars: 5-7g

Glycemic Index (GI): This meal has a low glycemic index due to the presence of fish, zucchini, and cherry tomatoes, making it a healthy and balanced choice.

Dover Sole Meunière with Parsley and Lemon

- *Difficulty Level:* ☐☐☐
- *Preparation Time: 15 minutes*
- *Cooking Time: 5 minutes*
- *Cooking Skill: Intermediate*

Ingredients for Two:

For the Dover Sole:

- *2 Dover sole fillets (or any other white fish fillets)*
- *Salt and black pepper, to taste*
- *All-purpose flour for dredging*
- *2 tablespoons unsalted butter*
- *2 tablespoons olive oil*

For the Meunière Sauce:

- *2 tablespoons unsalted butter*
- *2 tablespoons fresh lemon juice*
- *2 tablespoons fresh parsley, chopped*
- *Lemon wedges for garnish*

Instructions:

1. *Season the Dover sole fillets with salt and black pepper. Dredge them in flour, shaking off any excess.*

2. *Heat a large skillet over medium-high heat and add 2 tablespoons of butter and olive oil. When the butter is bubbling and starting to turn golden, add the sole fillets.*

3. *Cook the sole fillets for about 2-3 minutes on each side, or until they are golden brown and cooked through. The fish should easily flake with a fork when done. Transfer the cooked fillets to a serving plate and keep them warm.*

4. *In the same skillet, add an additional 2 tablespoons of butter and cook it until it turns brown (be careful not to burn it). This is the Meunière sauce.*

5. *Remove the skillet from the heat and add lemon juice and chopped parsley to the browned butter. Swirl to combine.*

6. *Pour the Meunière sauce over the cooked sole fillets.*

7. *Garnish with lemon wedges and extra chopped parsley.*

8. *Serve the Dover Sole Meunière hot, accompanied by your choice of side dishes.*

Nutritional Information (per serving):

Calories: Approximately 250-300 (may vary based on portion sizes)

Protein: 20-25g

Fat: 15-20g

Carbohydrates: 2-4g

Fiber: 1-2g

Sugars: 1g

Glycemic Index (GI): This meal is very low in carbohydrates and, therefore, has a low glycemic index. It's a delightful and balanced option for those looking for a light and elegant fish dish.

Sushi Bowl with Raw Tuna, Avocado, and Edamame

- *Difficulty Level: ☐☐*
- *Preparation Time: 15 minutes*
- *Cooking Time: 0 minutes*
- *Cooking Skill: Basic*

Ingredients for Two:

For the Sushi Bowl:

- *2 cups cooked sushi rice, cooled*
- *8 ounces (about 225g) fresh raw tuna, cubed*
- *1 ripe avocado, sliced*
- *1/2 cup shelled edamame, steamed and cooled*
- *1/4 cup thinly sliced nori (seaweed) sheets*
- *Pickled ginger, for garnish*

- *Wasabi and soy sauce, for serving*

For the Dressing:

- *2 tablespoons soy sauce*
- *1 tablespoon rice vinegar*
- *1 teaspoon sesame oil*
- *1 teaspoon honey or agave nectar*
- *1/2 teaspoon grated fresh ginger*
- *Sesame seeds, for garnish*

Instructions:

1. *In a small bowl, whisk together the soy sauce, rice vinegar, sesame oil, honey or agave nectar, and grated ginger. Set aside.*

2. *Divide the cooked sushi rice between two serving bowls.*

3. *Arrange the cubed raw tuna, sliced avocado, and steamed edamame on top of the rice in each bowl.*

4. *Drizzle the dressing over the ingredients in the bowls.*

5. *Sprinkle the sliced nori and sesame seeds over the top.*

6. *Garnish with pickled ginger.*

7. *Serve your sushi bowls with small dishes of wasabi and soy sauce on the side.*

8. *Enjoy your homemade sushi bowl!*

Nutritional Information (per serving):

Calories: Approximately 400-450 (may vary based on portion sizes)
Protein: 20-25g
Fat: 15-20g
Carbohydrates: 35-40g
Fiber: 5-6g
Sugars: 3-4g

Glycemic Index (GI): The glycemic index of this sushi bowl is relatively low, mainly because the sushi rice is the primary source of carbohydrates, and it has a moderate glycemic index. This meal offers a delightful combination of flavors and textures while keeping the glycemic load in check.

Seared Tuna with Soy Sauce and Sautéed Spinach

- *Difficulty Level:* ☐☐
- *Preparation Time: 20 minutes*
- *Cooking Time: 10 minutes*
- *Cooking Skill: Intermediate*

Ingredients for Two:

For the Seared Tuna:

- *2 tuna steaks (about 6-8 ounces each)*
- *2 tablespoons soy sauce*
- *1 tablespoon sesame oil*
- *1 teaspoon fresh ginger, minced*
- *1 clove garlic, minced*
- *1 tablespoon sesame seeds*
- *Salt and black pepper to taste*
- *2 tablespoons vegetable oil (for searing)*

For the Sautéed Spinach:

- 8-10 ounces fresh spinach leaves
- 2 cloves garlic, minced
- 1 tablespoon olive oil
- Salt and black pepper to taste

Instructions:

1. In a shallow dish, combine the soy sauce, sesame oil, minced ginger, minced garlic, sesame seeds, salt, and black pepper. Place the tuna steaks in the marinade, turning to coat. Allow them to marinate for about 10 minutes.

2. While the tuna is marinating, heat 2 tablespoons of vegetable oil in a large skillet over medium-high heat.

3. When the oil is hot, add the marinated tuna steaks. Sear for about 2-3 minutes per side for rare to medium-rare, or longer if you prefer your tuna more well-done. The cooking time depends on the thickness of the steaks.

4. Remove the seared tuna from the skillet and let it rest.

5. In the same skillet, add 1 tablespoon of olive oil and minced garlic. Sauté for about a minute until fragrant.

6. Add the fresh spinach to the skillet and cook, stirring, until it wilts and is tender. This should take just a few minutes.

7. Season the sautéed spinach with salt and black pepper to taste.

8. Serve the seared tuna on a bed of sautéed spinach.

9. Enjoy your seared tuna with soy sauce and sautéed spinach!

Nutritional Information (per serving):

Calories: Approximately 300-350 (may vary based on portion sizes)

Protein: 30-35g

Fat: 20-25g

Carbohydrates: 5-8g

Fiber: 2-3g

Sugars: 1-2g

Glycemic Index (GI): This dish has a low glycemic index as it primarily contains protein from the tuna and healthy fats from the sesame oil and olive oil. The spinach is also low in carbohydrates and has a minimal impact on blood sugar.

Mediterranean-Style Sea Bass en Papillote with Vegetables

- Difficulty Level: ☐☐
- Preparation Time: 20 minutes
- Cooking Time: 20 minutes
- Cooking Skill: Intermediate

Ingredients for Two:

For the Sea Bass en Papillote:

2 whole sea bass or branzino, gutted and scaled (about 12-16 ounces each)

2 tablespoons extra-virgin olive oil

4 cloves garlic, minced

1 lemon, thinly sliced

4 sprigs fresh rosemary

Salt and black pepper to taste

1/2 cup dry white wine (optional)

For the Mediterranean Vegetables:

1 red bell pepper, thinly sliced
1 yellow bell pepper, thinly sliced
1 small red onion, thinly sliced
1 zucchini, thinly sliced
1 cup cherry tomatoes, halved
2 tablespoons extra-virgin olive oil
1 tablespoon balsamic vinegar
2 cloves garlic, minced
1 teaspoon dried oregano
Salt and black pepper to taste

Instructions:

Preheat your oven to 400°F (200°C).

Prepare the Mediterranean vegetables: In a large bowl, combine the red and yellow bell peppers, red onion, zucchini, cherry tomatoes, olive oil, balsamic vinegar, minced garlic, dried oregano, salt, and black pepper. Toss to coat the vegetables in the seasoning.

Tear off two large sheets of parchment paper (approximately 18x24 inches each) and fold each sheet in half. This will create a crease down the center of each sheet.

1. Open up each parchment paper sheet and place a portion of the seasoned Mediterranean vegetables on one half of the sheet, close to the crease. Leave some space around the edges.

2. Place a sea bass on top of the vegetables. Season the fish with salt and black pepper, and stuff the cavity with minced garlic, lemon slices, and fresh rosemary.

If desired, drizzle about 1/4 cup of dry white wine over each sea bass.

1. Fold the other half of the parchment paper over the fish and vegetables. Starting at one end, make small overlapping folds along the edges to seal the packets completely. Place the packets on a baking sheet.

2. Bake in the preheated oven for about 18-20 minutes, until the sea bass is cooked through and the vegetables are tender.

3. Carefully open the parchment paper packets and serve the Mediterranean-style sea bass with vegetables directly from the packets.

Enjoy your Mediterranean-Style Sea Bass en Papillote with Vegetables!

Nutritional Information (per serving):

Calories: Approximately 350-400 (may vary based on portion sizes)
Protein: 30-35g
Fat: 20-25g
Carbohydrates: 15-20g
Fiber: 4-6g
Sugars: 6-8g

Glycemic Index (GI): This dish has a low glycemic index due to the primarily protein-based sea bass and the fiber-rich vegetables, which help stabilize blood sugar levels. The moderate amount of carbohydrates comes from the vegetables.

Grilled Jumbo Shrimp with Basmati Rice and Broccolini

- Difficulty Level: □□
- Preparation Time: 15 minutes
- Cooking Time: 15 minutes
- Cooking Skill: Intermediate

Ingredients for Two:

For the Grilled Jumbo Shrimp:
- 12 jumbo shrimp, peeled and deveined
- 2 tablespoons olive oil
- 2 cloves garlic, minced
- 1 lemon, zest and juice
- 1 teaspoon paprika
- Salt and black pepper to taste
- Wooden skewers (soaked in water)

For the Basmati Rice:
- 1 cup basmati rice
- 2 cups water
- Salt to taste

For the Broccolini:
- 1 bunch of broccolini
- 2 tablespoons olive oil
- 2 cloves garlic, minced
- Salt and black pepper to taste

Instructions:

1. Preheat your grill or grill pan to medium-high heat.

2. In a bowl, combine olive oil, minced garlic, lemon zest, lemon juice, paprika, salt, and black pepper. Toss the jumbo shrimp in this marinade to coat them evenly.

3. Thread the marinated shrimp onto wooden skewers.

4. Cook the shrimp on the preheated grill for about 2-3 minutes on each side, or until they turn pink and slightly charred. Remove them from the grill and set aside.

5. While the shrimp are cooking, rinse the basmati rice under cold water until the water runs clear. In a saucepan, combine the rice, water, and a pinch of salt. Bring to a boil, then reduce the heat to low, cover, and simmer for 12-15 minutes until the rice is tender and the water is absorbed. Remove from heat and let it rest, covered, for a few minutes.

6. In a separate pan, heat 2 tablespoons of olive oil over medium-high heat. Add minced garlic and broccolini, and sauté for about 5-7 minutes or until the broccolini is tender-crisp. Season with salt and black pepper.

7. Serve the grilled jumbo shrimp on a plate with cooked basmati rice and sautéed broccolini on the side.

8. Enjoy your Grilled Jumbo Shrimp with Basmati Rice and Broccolini!

Nutritional Information (per serving):

- Calories: Approximately 400-450 (may vary based on portion sizes)
- Protein: 25-30g
- Fat: 12-15g
- Carbohydrates: 45-50g

- Fiber: 2-4g
- Sugars: 2-4g

Glycemic Index (GI): This meal has a moderate glycemic index due to the presence of basmati rice. The broccolini and shrimp contribute to stabilizing blood sugar levels, and the overall glycemic index remains in the moderate range.

VEGETARIAN DISHES

Crispy Chickpea Patties with Yogurt Sauce and Cabbage Salad

- Difficulty Level: ☐☐
- Preparation Time: 20 minutes
- Cooking Time: 20 minutes
- Cooking Skill: Intermediate

Ingredients for Two:

For the Chickpea Patties:

- 1 can (15 oz) chickpeas, drained and rinsed
- 1/2 small red onion, finely chopped
- 2 cloves garlic, minced
- 1 teaspoon ground cumin
- 1/2 teaspoon ground coriander
- 1/4 teaspoon cayenne pepper (adjust to taste)
- 2 tablespoons fresh cilantro, chopped
- 2 tablespoons fresh parsley, chopped
- Salt and black pepper to taste
- 2 tablespoons all-purpose flour
- 2 tablespoons olive oil (for frying)

For the Yogurt Sauce:

- 1/2 cup Greek yogurt

- 1 tablespoon lemon juice
- 1 teaspoon fresh dill, chopped
- Salt and black pepper to taste

For the Cabbage Salad:

- 2 cups shredded green cabbage
- 1/2 cup shredded carrots
- 1/4 cup fresh mint leaves, chopped
- 2 tablespoons olive oil
- 1 tablespoon apple cider vinegar
- 1 teaspoon honey (optional)
- Salt and black pepper to taste

Instructions:

1. Place the drained chickpeas in a food processor and pulse until they are coarsely ground but not pureed. Transfer the ground chickpeas to a large bowl.

2. Add the chopped red onion, minced garlic, ground cumin, ground coriander, cayenne pepper, cilantro, parsley, salt, black pepper, and all-purpose flour to the chickpeas. Mix everything together until well combined.

3. Form the mixture into small patties, about 2 inches in diameter.

4. Heat the olive oil in a skillet over medium-high heat. Once the oil is hot, add the chickpea patties and cook for about 3-4 minutes on each side, or until they are golden brown and crispy. Remove from the skillet and place them on paper towels to drain any excess oil.

5. In a small bowl, mix together the Greek yogurt, lemon juice, fresh dill, salt, and

black pepper to prepare the yogurt sauce. Set aside.

6. In a separate bowl, combine the shredded green cabbage, shredded carrots, and chopped fresh mint for the cabbage salad.

7. In a small jar, whisk together olive oil, apple cider vinegar, honey (if using), salt, and black pepper to create the salad dressing. Pour this dressing over the cabbage mixture and toss to combine.

8. Serve the crispy chickpea patties with the yogurt sauce and the cabbage salad on the side.

9. Enjoy your Crispy Chickpea Patties with Yogurt Sauce and Cabbage Salad!

Nutritional Information (per serving):

Calories: Approximately 350-400 (may vary based on portion sizes)

Protein: 12-15g

Fat: 15-18g

Carbohydrates: 40-45g

Fiber: 8-10g

Sugars: 10-12g

Glycemic Index (GI): The overall glycemic index of this meal is low due to the chickpeas' moderate GI and the presence of vegetables and yogurt. This combination helps keep blood sugar levels stable.

Curry Tofu with Broccoli and Basmati Rice

- Difficulty Level: ☐☐

- Preparation Time: 15 minutes
- Cooking Time: 25 minutes
- Cooking Skill: Intermediate

Ingredients for Two:

For the Tofu Curry:

- 1 block (about 14 oz) firm tofu, cubed
- 2 tablespoons vegetable oil
- 1 small onion, finely chopped
- 2 cloves garlic, minced
- 1 tablespoon fresh ginger, minced
- 2 tablespoons curry powder
- 1 can (14 oz) diced tomatoes
- 1 can (14 oz) coconut milk
- 2 cups broccoli florets
- Salt and black pepper to taste
- Fresh cilantro leaves for garnish (optional)

For the Basmati Rice:

- 1 cup basmati rice
- 2 cups water
- 1/2 teaspoon salt

Instructions:

1. Start by cooking the basmati rice. Rinse the rice in a fine-mesh strainer until the water runs clear. In a medium saucepan, combine the rinsed rice, water, and salt. Bring to a boil, then reduce the heat to low, cover, and simmer for about 15-18 minutes or until the rice is tender and the water is absorbed. Remove from heat and let it sit, covered, for 5 minutes. Fluff the rice with a fork before serving.

2. While the rice is cooking, prepare the tofu curry. Heat the vegetable oil in a

large skillet or pan over medium heat. Add the chopped onion and cook until it becomes translucent.

3. Add the minced garlic and ginger to the skillet and cook for another minute until fragrant.

4. Stir in the curry powder and cook for about 2 minutes, allowing the spices to bloom.

5. Add the diced tomatoes and their juice to the pan. Stir well and let it simmer for 5 minutes.

6. Pour in the coconut milk and mix it with the tomato mixture. Allow it to simmer for another 5 minutes, stirring occasionally.

7. Add the cubed tofu to the sauce and let it simmer for about 10 minutes, or until the tofu is heated through and absorbs some of the flavors.

8. In the last 5 minutes of cooking, add the broccoli florets to the curry. Cook until the broccoli is tender but still crisp.

9. Season the curry with salt and black pepper to taste.

10. Serve the tofu curry over the cooked basmati rice. Garnish with fresh cilantro leaves if desired.

11. Enjoy your Tofu Curry with Broccoli and Basmati Rice!

Nutritional Information (per serving):

Calories: Approximately 400-450 (may vary based on portion sizes)

Protein: 12-15g

Fat: 20-25g

Carbohydrates: 40-45g

Fiber: 6-8g

Sugars: 6-8g

Glycemic Index (GI): The overall glycemic index of this meal is moderate due to the presence of rice and some vegetables. The tofu and curry components contribute to balancing blood sugar levels.

Chickpea Patties with Yogurt Sauce and Cabbage Salad

- *Difficulty Level:* ☐☐
- *Preparation Time: 20 minutes*
- *Cooking Time: 15 minutes*
- *Cooking Skill: Easy to Medium*

Ingredients for Two:

For the Chickpea Patties:

- *1 can (14 oz) chickpeas, drained and rinsed*
- *1/2 small red onion, finely chopped*
- *2 cloves garlic, minced*
- *1 teaspoon ground cumin*
- *1 teaspoon ground coriander*
- *1/4 cup fresh cilantro, chopped*
- *1/4 cup fresh parsley, chopped*
- *1/2 teaspoon salt*
- *1/4 teaspoon black pepper*
- *1/2 cup breadcrumbs*
- *1 egg*
- *2 tablespoons olive oil*

For the Yogurt Sauce:

- *1/2 cup Greek yogurt*
- *1 tablespoon lemon juice*
- *1 clove garlic, minced*
- *1/4 teaspoon ground cumin*
- *Salt and black pepper to taste*

For the Cabbage Salad:

- *2 cups shredded green cabbage*
- *1 small carrot, grated*
- *1/4 cup red bell pepper, thinly sliced*
- *2 tablespoons fresh cilantro, chopped*
- *2 tablespoons fresh parsley, chopped*
- *1 tablespoon olive oil*
- *1 tablespoon white wine vinegar*
- *Salt and black pepper to taste*

Instructions:

1. *Start by making the chickpea patties. In a food processor, combine the chickpeas, red onion, minced garlic, ground cumin, ground coriander, fresh cilantro, fresh parsley, salt, and black pepper. Pulse until the mixture is well combined but still slightly chunky.*

2. *Transfer the chickpea mixture to a mixing bowl. Add the breadcrumbs and egg, and mix until all ingredients are fully incorporated.*

3. *Shape the mixture into small patties (about 8 patties) and place them on a baking sheet.*

4. *Heat the olive oil in a skillet over medium heat. Once hot, add the chickpea patties and cook for about 3-4 minutes on each side or until they are golden brown and firm.*

5. *While the patties are cooking, prepare the yogurt sauce. In a bowl, mix together the Greek yogurt, lemon juice, minced garlic, ground cumin, salt, and black pepper.*

6. *For the cabbage salad, in a separate bowl, combine the shredded cabbage, grated carrot, red bell pepper, fresh cilantro, fresh parsley, olive oil, white wine vinegar, salt, and black pepper. Toss until everything is well coated.*

7. *Serve the chickpea patties on a plate with a dollop of yogurt sauce and a side of cabbage salad.*

8. *Enjoy your Chickpea Patties with Yogurt Sauce and Cabbage Salad!*

Nutritional Information (per serving):

Calories: Approximately 350-400 (may vary based on portion sizes)

Protein: 10-12g

Fat: 15-18g

Carbohydrates: 40-45g

Fiber: 6-8g

Sugars: 6-8g

Glycemic Index (GI): The overall glycemic index of this meal is moderate due to the presence of chickpeas and vegetables. The patties have a lower GI compared to some other starchy foods. The salad and yogurt components help balance blood sugar levels.

Light Eggplant Parmesan with Mixed Salad

- *Difficulty Level:* ☐☐

- Preparation Time: 30 minutes
- Cooking Time: 40 minutes
- Cooking Skill: Medium

Ingredients for Two:

For the Light Eggplant Parmesan:

- 2 small or 1 large eggplant, sliced into 1/2-inch rounds
- 2 cups marinara sauce (you can use a low-sugar or homemade version)
- 1 cup part-skim mozzarella cheese, shredded
- 1/2 cup Parmesan cheese, grated
- 1/2 cup whole-wheat breadcrumbs
- 1/4 cup fresh basil leaves
- 1 tablespoon olive oil
- Salt and black pepper to taste

For the Mixed Salad:

- 4 cups mixed salad greens (e.g., lettuce, arugula, spinach)
- 1 cup cherry tomatoes, halved
- 1/4 red onion, thinly sliced
- 1/4 cup balsamic vinaigrette dressing (you can use a light or homemade version)

Instructions:

1. Preheat your oven to 375°F (190°C).

2. In a large bowl, place the eggplant slices, drizzle with olive oil, season with salt and black pepper, and toss to coat.

3. Arrange the eggplant slices on a baking sheet lined with parchment paper. Bake for about 15-20 minutes or until the eggplant is tender and slightly golden. You may need to flip them halfway through.

4. In a separate bowl, combine the breadcrumbs and grated Parmesan cheese.

5. Once the eggplant is done, remove it from the oven. Increase the oven temperature to 400°F (200°C).

6. In a baking dish, spread a thin layer of marinara sauce. Place a layer of baked eggplant slices on top. Add some mozzarella cheese, Parmesan-breadcrumb mixture, and fresh basil leaves.

7. Repeat the layering process until all ingredients are used, ending with a layer of marinara sauce and a generous sprinkle of cheese and breadcrumbs.

8. Bake the eggplant Parmesan in the preheated oven for about 20-25 minutes or until it's bubbly and the cheese is golden brown.

9. While the eggplant Parmesan is baking, prepare the mixed salad. In a large salad bowl, combine the salad greens, cherry tomatoes, and red onion. Drizzle with balsamic vinaigrette dressing and toss to coat.

10. Once the eggplant Parmesan is done, remove it from the oven and let it cool for a few minutes.

11. Serve the light eggplant Parmesan with a side of mixed salad.

12. Enjoy your Light Eggplant Parmesan with Mixed Salad!

Nutritional Information (per serving):

Calories: Approximately 450-500 (may vary based on portion sizes)

Protein: 18-20g

Fat: 18-20g

Carbohydrates: 45-50g

Fiber: 8-10g

Sugars: 8-10g

Glycemic Index (GI): The overall glycemic index of this meal is moderate, with the eggplant having a low GI and salad being very low in GI. The use of whole-wheat breadcrumbs contributes to a moderate GI.

Quinoa with Mushrooms and Goat Cheese

- *Difficulty Level:* ☐ ☐
- *Preparation Time: 25 minutes*
- *Cooking Time: 20 minutes*
- *Cooking Skill: Medium*

Ingredients for Two:

For the Quinoa:

- *1 cup quinoa*
- *2 cups vegetable broth*
- *1 tablespoon olive oil*
- *1 small onion, finely chopped*
- *2 cloves garlic, minced*
- *8 ounces (about 225g) mushrooms (such as cremini or button), sliced*
- *Salt and black pepper to taste*
- *2 ounces (about 60g) soft goat cheese*
- *Fresh parsley, chopped, for garnish*

Instructions:

1. *Rinse the quinoa under cold running water. In a medium saucepan, combine the quinoa and vegetable broth. Bring to a boil, then reduce the heat to low, cover, and let it simmer for about 15 minutes, or until the quinoa is cooked and the liquid is absorbed. Remove from heat and let it sit for 5 minutes. Fluff the quinoa with a fork.*

2. *While the quinoa is cooking, heat olive oil in a large skillet over medium heat. Add the chopped onion and cook until it becomes translucent, about 3 minutes.*

3. *Add the minced garlic and sliced mushrooms to the skillet. Cook, stirring occasionally, until the mushrooms are tender and browned, about 8-10 minutes. Season with salt and black pepper to taste.*

4. *Add the cooked quinoa to the skillet with the mushroom mixture. Stir everything together and cook for an additional 2-3 minutes to heat through.*

5. *Crumble the soft goat cheese into the skillet and gently fold it into the quinoa and mushrooms until it's melted and combined.*

6. *Remove from heat, and garnish with chopped fresh parsley.*

7. *Serve the quinoa with mushrooms and goat cheese hot as a delightful side dish or a vegetarian main course.*

8. Enjoy your Quinoa with Mushrooms and Goat Cheese!

Nutritional Information (per serving):

Calories: Approximately 350-400 (may vary based on portion sizes)

Protein: 13-15g

Fat: 11-13g

Carbohydrates: 50-55g

Fiber: 7-9g

Sugars: 4-6g

Glycemic Index (GI): Quinoa has a low to moderate GI, which means it can help maintain more stable blood sugar levels compared to high-GI foods. The addition of mushrooms and goat cheese doesn't significantly impact the overall GI of this dish.

Polenta with Grilled Vegetables and Basil Pesto

- Difficulty Level: ☐☐
- Preparation Time: 20 minutes
- Cooking Time: 25 minutes
- Cooking Skill: Medium

Ingredients for Two:

For the Polenta:

- 1 cup polenta (cornmeal)
- 4 cups water
- Salt, to taste
- 1/4 cup grated Parmesan cheese
- 2 tablespoons unsalted butter

For the Grilled Vegetables:

- 1 small zucchini, sliced lengthwise
- 1 red bell pepper, cut into large strips
- 1 yellow bell pepper, cut into large strips
- 1 small red onion, cut into thick rings
- 2 tablespoons olive oil
- Salt and black pepper, to taste

For the Basil Pesto:

- 2 cups fresh basil leaves
- 1/4 cup pine nuts
- 2 cloves garlic
- 1/2 cup grated Parmesan cheese
- 1/2 cup extra-virgin olive oil
- Salt and black pepper, to taste

Instructions:

Prepare the Polenta:

1. In a large saucepan, bring 4 cups of water to a boil.
2. Gradually whisk in the polenta, stirring constantly to prevent lumps.
3. Reduce the heat to low and continue to cook the polenta, stirring frequently, for about 20-25 minutes until it's thick and creamy.
4. Stir in the grated Parmesan cheese and butter. Season with salt to taste. Keep warm.

Grill the Vegetables:

5. Preheat your grill or grill pan over medium-high heat.
6. Toss the sliced zucchini, bell peppers, and red onion with olive oil, salt, and black pepper.
7. Grill the vegetables until they are tender and have grill marks, about 3-4 minutes

per side. Remove them from the grill and set aside.

Make the Basil Pesto:

8. In a food processor, combine the basil leaves, pine nuts, garlic, and grated Parmesan cheese.
9. Pulse until the ingredients are finely chopped.
10. With the food processor running, slowly drizzle in the extra-virgin olive oil until the pesto reaches your desired consistency.
11. Season with salt and black pepper to taste.

Assemble the Dish:

12. Spoon a generous portion of polenta onto each plate.
13. Arrange the grilled vegetables on top of the polenta.
14. Drizzle the basil pesto over the grilled vegetables.

15. Serve your Polenta with Grilled Vegetables and Basil Pesto as a delicious and visually appealing meal.

16. Enjoy your culinary creation!

Nutritional Information (per serving):

Calories: Approximately 500-600 (may vary based on portion sizes)

Protein: 10-12g

Fat: 30-35g

Carbohydrates: 50-60g

Fiber: 6-8g

Sugars: 6-8g

Glycemic Index (GI): Polenta has a moderate GI, which can vary depending on the specific type and processing. Grilled vegetables and pesto have minimal impact on the overall GI of this dish.

Stuffed Butternut Squash with Wild Rice and Walnuts

- *Difficulty Level:* □□
- *Preparation Time: 30 minutes*
- *Cooking Time: 1 hour*
- *Cooking Skill: Medium*

Ingredients for Two:

For the Stuffed Butternut Squash:

- *1 small butternut squash, halved and seeds removed*
- *1 cup wild rice*
- *2 cups vegetable broth*
- *1/2 cup chopped walnuts*
- *1/4 cup dried cranberries*
- *1 small red onion, finely chopped*
- *2 cloves garlic, minced*
- *2 tablespoons olive oil*
- *Salt and black pepper, to taste*
- *Fresh parsley, for garnish (optional)*

Instructions:

1. Preheat your oven to 375°F (190°C).

2. Prepare the Butternut Squash:

3. Cut the butternut squash in half lengthwise and scoop out the seeds.

4. Place the squash halves on a baking sheet, cut side up.

5. Drizzle with 1 tablespoon of olive oil, and season with salt and black pepper.

Roast the squash:

6. Roast the butternut squash in the preheated oven for about 45 minutes to 1 hour or until the flesh is tender when pierced with a fork.

Cook the Wild Rice:

7. While the squash is roasting, rinse the wild rice under cold water.
8. In a saucepan, bring 2 cups of vegetable broth to a boil.
9. Add the rinsed wild rice to the boiling broth, reduce the heat, cover, and simmer for about 30-40 minutes or until the rice is tender and the liquid is absorbed.
10. Fluff the cooked rice with a fork and set it aside.

Prepare the Filling:

11. In a skillet, heat 1 tablespoon of olive oil over medium heat.
12. Add the chopped red onion and garlic and sauté until they become translucent.
13. Stir in the cooked wild rice, chopped walnuts, and dried cranberries.
14. Cook for an additional 2-3 minutes, stirring to combine all the ingredients. Season with salt and black pepper.

Assemble the Stuffed Squash:

15. Once the butternut squash is tender and fully roasted, remove it from the oven.
16. Carefully fill each squash half with the wild rice mixture.

17. Return to the oven:

18. Place the stuffed squash back in the oven for an additional 10-15 minutes to heat through.

Garnish and Serve:

19. Garnish with fresh parsley, if desired.
20. Serve your Stuffed Butternut Squash with Wild Rice and Walnuts as a delightful, wholesome meal.

21. Enjoy your culinary creation!

Nutritional Information (per serving):

Calories: Approximately 400-500 (may vary based on portion sizes)

Protein: 10-12g

Fat: 15-20g

Carbohydrates: 65-75g

Fiber: 10-12g

Sugars: 10-12g

Glycemic Index (GI): Wild rice has a moderate GI, while butternut squash has a low GI. The overall GI of this dish remains moderate

Vegetarian Pad Thai with Tofu and Vegetables

- Difficulty Level: ☐ ☐
- Preparation Time: 20 minutes
- Cooking Time: 15 minutes
- Cooking Skill: Medium

Ingredients for Two:

- *For the Pad Thai Sauce:*

- *3 tablespoons tamarind paste*
- *2 tablespoons soy sauce*
- *2 tablespoons brown sugar*
- *1 tablespoon lime juice*
- *1-2 teaspoons chili sauce (adjust to taste)*
- *1 clove garlic, minced*

For the Pad Thai:

- *6 oz (about 170g) rice noodles*
- *7 oz (about 200g) extra-firm tofu, pressed and cubed*
- *2 tablespoons vegetable oil*
- *1 small carrot, julienned*
- *1 bell pepper, thinly sliced*
- *1 cup bean sprouts*
- *2 green onions, chopped*
- *2 cloves garlic, minced*
- *1/4 cup roasted peanuts, chopped*
- *Lime wedges and cilantro, for garnish (optional)*

Instructions:

Prepare the Rice Noodles:

1. *Cook the rice noodles according to the package instructions. Drain and set them aside.*

Prepare the Pad Thai Sauce:

2. *In a small bowl, whisk together the tamarind paste, soy sauce, brown sugar, lime juice, chili sauce, and minced garlic. Adjust the ingredients to achieve your preferred balance of sweet, sour, and spicy. Set the sauce aside.*

Cook the Tofu:

3. *Heat 1 tablespoon of vegetable oil in a large skillet or wok over medium-high heat.*
4. *Add the tofu cubes and cook until they become golden brown and crispy on all sides. Remove them from the pan and set them aside.*

Sauté the Vegetables:

5. *In the same skillet, add the remaining 1 tablespoon of vegetable oil.*
6. *Add the julienned carrot, sliced bell pepper, bean sprouts, green onions, and minced garlic.*
7. *Sauté the vegetables for a few minutes until they become tender but still crisp.*

Combine and Toss:

8. *Return the cooked rice noodles and crispy tofu to the skillet with the sautéed vegetables.*
9. *Pour the Pad Thai sauce over the ingredients.*
10. *Gently toss everything together to ensure the noodles and tofu are well coated with the sauce. Continue cooking for a few minutes to heat through.*

Serve:

11. *Serve the Vegetarian Pad Thai on plates or in bowls.*
12. *Garnish with chopped roasted peanuts and, if desired, lime wedges and cilantro.*

13. *Enjoy your delicious Vegetarian Pad Thai with Tofu and Vegetables!*

Nutritional Information (per serving):

Calories: Approximately 400-500 (may vary based on portion sizes)
Protein: 10-15g
Fat: 15-20g
Carbohydrates: 50-60g
Fiber: 4-6g
Sugars: 10-15g

Glycemic Index (GI): The glycemic index can vary depending on the rice noodles and amount of sugar used. However, traditional Pad Thai has a moderate GI due to the rice noodles and sugar content.

Spinach, Cherry Tomato, and Feta Frittata

- *Difficulty Level: ☐☐*
- *Preparation Time: 15 minutes*
- *Cooking Time: 15 minutes*
- *Cooking Skill: Easy*

Ingredients for Two:

- *4 large eggs*
- *2 cups fresh spinach, chopped*
- *1/2 cup cherry tomatoes, halved*
- *1/4 cup crumbled feta cheese*
- *1/4 cup milk (you can use regular milk or a dairy-free alternative)*
- *1 tablespoon olive oil*
- *1/4 teaspoon salt*
- *1/4 teaspoon black pepper*
- *1/4 teaspoon dried oregano (optional)*

Instructions:

1. *Preheat the Oven:*

2. *Preheat your oven's broiler on a low setting.*

3. *Whisk the Eggs:*

4. *In a bowl, whisk the eggs together with the milk, salt, pepper, and dried oregano (if using). Set aside.*

5. *Sauté the Spinach:*

6. *Heat the olive oil in an oven-safe skillet over medium heat.*
7. *Add the chopped spinach and sauté for about 2-3 minutes, or until it wilts.*

8. *Add the Tomatoes and Feta:*

9. *Add the halved cherry tomatoes and crumbled feta to the skillet. Stir to combine the ingredients.*

10. *Pour the Egg Mixture:*

11. *Pour the whisked egg mixture into the skillet, ensuring it evenly covers the spinach, tomatoes, and feta.*

12. *Cook on the Stovetop:*

13. *Cook the frittata on the stovetop for about 4-5 minutes, or until the edges start to set. The center should still be slightly runny.*

14. *Broil in the Oven:*

15. *Place the skillet under the broiler and broil the frittata for approximately 4-5 minutes. Keep an eye on it to avoid*

overcooking. The frittata is ready when it's puffed up and golden brown on top.

16. Serve:

17. Carefully remove the skillet from the oven (use an oven mitt as the handle will be hot).
18. Let the frittata cool for a few minutes before slicing it into wedges.

19. Enjoy your Spinach, Cherry Tomato, and Feta Frittata!

Nutritional Information (per serving):

Calories: Approximately 220-250 (may vary based on portion sizes)
Protein: 14-16g
Fat: 16-18g
Carbohydrates: 5-7g
Fiber: 1-2g
Sugars: 3-4g

Glycemic Index (GI): Frittatas, in general, have a low glycemic index because they are not based on high-carb ingredients. The ingredients used in this frittata should also have a low GI.

Portobello Mushrooms Stuffed with Whole Grain Rice and Low-Fat Cheese

- Difficulty Level: ☐ ☐
- Preparation Time: 20 minutes
- Cooking Time: 30 minutes
- Cooking Skill: Medium

Ingredients for Two:

- 4 large Portobello mushrooms
- 1 cup whole grain rice
- 2 cups water or vegetable broth
- 1/2 cup low-fat cheese (such as mozzarella or cheddar), shredded
- 1/4 cup red bell pepper, finely chopped
- 1/4 cup red onion, finely chopped
- 2 cloves garlic, minced
- 2 tablespoons fresh parsley, chopped
- 2 tablespoons olive oil
- Salt and pepper to taste
- Optional: a sprinkle of grated Parmesan cheese (for topping)

Instructions:

1. Prepare the Rice:

2. Rinse the whole grain rice under cold water until the water runs clear.
3. In a medium saucepan, bring 2 cups of water or vegetable broth to a boil. Add the rinsed rice, reduce heat to low, cover, and simmer for about 15-20 minutes, or until the rice is tender and the liquid is absorbed. Remove from heat and let it cool.

4. Prepare the Mushrooms:

5. Preheat your oven to 375°F (190°C).
6. Remove the stems from the Portobello mushrooms and gently scrape out the gills using a spoon. Brush the mushrooms with a bit of olive oil on both sides and place them on a baking sheet.

7. Make the Filling:

8. In a skillet, heat 1 tablespoon of olive oil over medium heat. Add the chopped red onion, red bell pepper, and garlic.

Sauté until the vegetables are softened and aromatic, about 3-4 minutes. Remove from heat.

9. Assemble the Stuffed Mushrooms:

10. In a mixing bowl, combine the cooked rice, sautéed vegetables, shredded low-fat cheese, and chopped parsley. Mix well.

11. Season the mixture with salt and pepper to taste.

12. Stuff the Mushrooms:

13. Generously fill each Portobello mushroom cap with the rice and vegetable mixture, pressing it down slightly. You can mound the filling as needed.

14. Bake:

15. Place the stuffed Portobello mushrooms in the preheated oven and bake for approximately 20-25 minutes or until the mushrooms are tender and the cheese is melted.

16. Optional Topping:

17. If desired, sprinkle a bit of grated Parmesan cheese over the stuffed mushrooms during the last 5 minutes of baking for added flavor.

18. Serve:

19. Carefully remove the stuffed mushrooms from the oven.

20. Plate your Portobello mushrooms stuffed with whole grain rice and low-fat cheese.

21. Enjoy your Portobello Mushrooms Stuffed with Whole Grain Rice and Low-Fat Cheese!

Nutritional Information (per serving):

Calories: Approximately 300-350 (may vary based on portion sizes)

Protein: 12-14g

Fat: 8-10g

Carbohydrates: 50-55g

Fiber: 6-8g

Sugars: 3-4g

Glycemic Index (GI): This dish has a low to moderate glycemic index, primarily from the whole grain rice. The vegetables and mushrooms have a minimal impact on blood sugar levels.

Couscous with Chickpeas, Grilled Vegetables, and Tahini Sauce

- Difficulty Level: ▢▢
- Preparation Time: 20 minutes
- Cooking Time: 15 minutes
- Cooking Skill: Medium

Ingredients for Two:

- For the Couscous and Chickpeas:

- 1 cup couscous
- 1 1/4 cups boiling water
- 1 can (15 oz) chickpeas, drained and rinsed

- *2 tablespoons olive oil*
- *1/2 teaspoon ground cumin*
- *Salt and pepper to taste*

For the Grilled Vegetables:

- *1 zucchini, sliced into thin strips*
- *1 red bell pepper, sliced into thin strips*
- *1 small eggplant, sliced into thin rounds*
- *2 tablespoons olive oil*
- *Salt and pepper to taste*

For the Tahini Sauce:

- *1/4 cup tahini*
- *2 tablespoons lemon juice*
- *2 tablespoons water*
- *1 clove garlic, minced*
- *Salt and pepper to taste*

Instructions:

1. *Grill the Vegetables:*

2. *Preheat your grill or grill pan over medium-high heat.*
3. *In a large bowl, toss the sliced zucchini, red bell pepper, and eggplant with 2 tablespoons of olive oil. Season with salt and pepper.*
4. *Grill the vegetables until they're tender and have grill marks, about 2-3 minutes per side for the zucchini and red bell pepper, and 3-4 minutes per side for the eggplant. Remove from the grill.*

5. *Prepare the Couscous and Chickpeas:*

6. *Place the couscous in a large heatproof bowl. Pour the boiling water over the couscous. Cover the bowl with a lid or*

plastic wrap and let it sit for 5 minutes. Fluff the couscous with a fork.

7. *In a skillet, heat 2 tablespoons of olive oil over medium heat. Add the drained chickpeas and ground cumin. Sauté until the chickpeas are slightly crispy and coated with the cumin, about 5 minutes. Season with salt and pepper.*

8. *Make the Tahini Sauce:*

9. *In a small bowl, whisk together the tahini, lemon juice, water, minced garlic, salt, and pepper until the sauce is smooth and creamy. Adjust the consistency with more water if needed.*

10. *Assemble the Dish:*

11. *Place a portion of couscous on each plate.*
12. *Top the couscous with the sautéed chickpeas and grilled vegetables.*

13. *Drizzle with Tahini Sauce:*

14. *Drizzle the prepared tahini sauce over the couscous, chickpeas, and grilled vegetables.*

15. *Serve:*

16. *Serve your couscous with chickpeas, grilled vegetables, and tahini sauce immediately.*

17. *Enjoy your Couscous with Chickpeas, Grilled Vegetables, and Tahini Sauce!*

Nutritional Information (per serving):

Calories: Approximately 450-500 (may vary based on portion sizes)

Protein: 12-14g

Fat: 16-18g

Carbohydrates: 65-70g

Fiber: 10-12g

Sugars: 6-8g

Glycemic Index (GI): This dish has a moderate glycemic index, mainly from the couscous and chickpeas. The vegetables and tahini sauce have minimal impacts on blood sugar levels.

OVEN-ROASTED VEGETABLE

Roasted Asparagus with Sliced Almonds

- *Difficulty Level:* ☐☐
- *Preparation Time: 10 minutes*
- *Cooking Time: 12-15 minutes*
- *Cooking Skill: Easy*

Ingredients for Two:

- *1 bunch of fresh asparagus spears*
- *2 tablespoons olive oil*
- *Salt and black pepper to taste*
- *2 tablespoons sliced almonds*
- *1 lemon, zested*
- *1-2 cloves of garlic, minced (optional)*

Instructions:

1. *Preheat the Oven:*

2. *Preheat your oven to 425°F (220°C).*

3. *Prepare the Asparagus:*

4. *Wash the asparagus spears and trim off the tough ends. You can do this by holding one end of the asparagus and bending it until it naturally snaps at the point where it becomes tender. Discard the tough ends.*

5. *Season the Asparagus:*

6. *Place the asparagus on a baking sheet. Drizzle 2 tablespoons of olive oil over the asparagus and toss them to coat evenly. Season with salt and black pepper to taste.*

7. *You can also add minced garlic for extra flavor if you like.*

8. *Roast the Asparagus:*

9. *Spread the asparagus out in a single layer on the baking sheet. Roast in the preheated oven for about 12-15 minutes or until they are tender but still slightly crisp. Cooking time may vary depending on the thickness of the asparagus spears, so keep an eye on them.*

10. *Toast the Almonds:*

11. *While the asparagus is roasting, place the sliced almonds in a dry skillet over medium-low heat. Toast them, stirring frequently until they turn golden brown and fragrant. This should take about 3-5 minutes.*

12. *Zest the Lemon:*

13. *Using a zester or a fine grater, zest the lemon to create lemon zest.*

14. Assemble the Dish:

15. Once the asparagus is done roasting, transfer them to a serving platter.
16. Sprinkle the toasted sliced almonds and lemon zest over the asparagus.

17. Serve:

18. Serve your roasted asparagus with sliced almonds and lemon zest immediately. Enjoy!

Nutritional Information (per serving):

Calories: Approximately 100-120 (may vary based on portion sizes)

Protein: 3-4g

Fat: 9-10g

Carbohydrates: 4-6g

Fiber: 2-3g

Sugars: 2-3g

Glycemic Index (GI): Asparagus has a very low glycemic index, which means it has minimal impact on blood sugar levels. The almonds and olive oil also contribute to a slow and steady release of energy.

Baked Zucchini with Herbs

- Difficulty Level: ☐☐
- Preparation Time: 10 minutes
- Cooking Time: 20-25 minutes
- Cooking Skill: Easy

Ingredients for Two:

- 2 medium zucchinis
- 2 tablespoons olive oil
- 2 cloves of garlic, minced

- 1 tablespoon fresh herbs (such as rosemary, thyme, or oregano), chopped
- Salt and black pepper to taste
- Grated Parmesan cheese (optional)

Instructions:

1. Preheat the Oven:

2. Preheat your oven to 400°F (200°C).

3. Prepare the Zucchini:

4. Wash the zucchinis and trim off the ends. Slice them into rounds or sticks, depending on your preference.

5. Season the Zucchini:

6. In a bowl, combine the zucchini slices or sticks, olive oil, minced garlic, chopped fresh herbs, salt, and black pepper. Toss to coat the zucchini evenly with the seasonings.

7. Arrange on a Baking Sheet:

8. Spread the seasoned zucchini on a baking sheet in a single layer.

9. Bake:

10. Place the baking sheet in the preheated oven and bake for 20-25 minutes, or until the zucchini becomes tender and slightly golden at the edges. Be sure to flip the zucchini halfway through the cooking time for even roasting.

11. Serve:

12. Once the zucchini is done, remove it from the oven and transfer it to a serving platter. If desired, sprinkle some grated Parmesan cheese over the top before serving.

Nutritional Information (per serving):

Calories: Approximately 80-100 (may vary based on portion sizes)
Protein: 2-3g
Fat: 7-9g
Carbohydrates: 4-6g
Fiber: 2-3g
Sugars: 2-3g

Glycemic Index (GI): Zucchini has a very low glycemic index, meaning it has minimal impact on blood sugar levels. The olive oil and herbs don't significantly affect the GI, making this a healthy and blood sugar-friendly dish.

Baked Stuffed Sun-Dried Tomatoes with Quinoa and Vegetables

- *Difficulty Level:* ☐☐
- *Preparation Time: 15 minutes*
- *Cooking Time: 30 minutes*
- *Cooking Skill: Intermediate*

Ingredients for Two:

- *6-8 sun-dried tomatoes, dried or in oil*
- *1/2 cup quinoa*
- *1 cup water*
- *1/2 cup mixed vegetables (e.g., bell peppers, zucchini, or spinach), finely chopped*
- *1/4 cup crumbled feta cheese (optional)*

- *2 tablespoons olive oil*
- *2 cloves garlic, minced*
- *1 teaspoon dried herbs (such as basil, oregano, or thyme)*
- *Salt and black pepper to taste*
- *Fresh basil leaves for garnish (optional)*

Instructions:

1. *Preheat the Oven:*

2. *Preheat your oven to 375°F (190°C).*

3. *Prepare the Sun-Dried Tomatoes:*

4. *If you're using dried sun-dried tomatoes, rehydrate them by soaking in hot water for about 10 minutes. Drain and pat them dry. If you're using sun-dried tomatoes in oil, pat them dry.*

5. *Cook the Quinoa:*

6. *In a saucepan, combine the quinoa and water. Bring to a boil, then reduce the heat, cover, and simmer for about 15 minutes, or until the quinoa is cooked and the water is absorbed.*

7. *Prepare the Filling:*

8. *In a skillet, heat 2 tablespoons of olive oil over medium heat. Add the minced garlic and cook for a minute until fragrant. Add the finely chopped mixed vegetables and sauté until they soften, about 5-7 minutes. Season with dried herbs, salt, and black pepper. Once the quinoa is cooked, add it to the skillet with the vegetables and mix well. If you're using feta cheese, fold it into the quinoa and vegetable mixture.*

9. *Stuff the Tomatoes:*

10. *Gently open each sun-dried tomato and stuff them with the quinoa and vegetable mixture. Press the filling down with a spoon to ensure they're tightly packed.*

11. *Bake:*

12. *Place the stuffed sun-dried tomatoes on a baking sheet and bake in the preheated oven for about 15-20 minutes, or until they're heated through and the edges of the tomatoes become slightly crispy.*

13. *Serve:*

14. *Remove the stuffed sun-dried tomatoes from the oven and let them cool slightly. Garnish with fresh basil leaves if desired.*

15. *Enjoy:*

16. *Serve your baked stuffed sun-dried tomatoes with quinoa and vegetables as an appetizer or side dish. They can also be enjoyed as a light main course.*

17. *Nutritional Information (per serving, without feta cheese):*

Calories: Approximately 180-220 (may vary based on portion sizes)

Protein: 5-7g

Fat: 7-9g

Carbohydrates: 25-30g

Fiber: 4-5g

Sugars: 2-3g

Glycemic Index (GI): The quinoa and vegetables in this dish provide a moderate GI, making it a balanced and nutritious option for your meal.

Baked Carrots with Ginger and Honey

- *Difficulty Level:* ☐☐
- *Preparation Time: 10 minutes*
- *Cooking Time: 25-30 minutes*
- *Cooking Skill: Easy*

Ingredients for Two:

- *4-5 large carrots, peeled and cut into sticks or rounds*
- *2 tablespoons olive oil*
- *1 tablespoon honey*
- *1 teaspoon freshly grated ginger*
- *Salt and black pepper to taste*
- *Fresh parsley leaves for garnish (optional)*

Instructions:

1. *Preheat the Oven:*

2. *Preheat your oven to 375°F (190°C).*

3. *Prepare the Carrots:*

4. *Peel the carrots and cut them into sticks or rounds, whichever you prefer. Make sure the pieces are of similar size to ensure even cooking.*

5. *Make the Ginger Honey Glaze:*

6. In a small bowl, mix together the olive oil, honey, and freshly grated ginger. This will be your glaze.

7. Coat the Carrots:

8. Place the carrot pieces on a baking sheet. Drizzle the ginger honey glaze over the carrots and toss them to ensure they are evenly coated. Season with salt and black pepper to taste.

9. Bake:

10. Put the baking sheet in the preheated oven and bake for about 25-30 minutes, or until the carrots are tender and slightly caramelized. You can toss the carrots once or twice during baking for even cooking.

11. Garnish and Serve:

12. Remove the baked carrots from the oven. If desired, garnish with fresh parsley leaves for a pop of color and flavor.

13. Enjoy:

14. Serve your baked carrots with ginger and honey as a delicious side dish to complement your main course. They make a sweet and savory addition to your meal.

Nutritional Information (per serving):

Calories: Approximately 120-140 (may vary based on portion sizes)
Protein: 1-2g
Fat: 7-8g

Carbohydrates: 14-16g
Fiber: 3-4g
Sugars: 10-12g

Glycemic Index (GI): The glycemic index of this dish is relatively low, thanks to the carrots and their natural sugars. The ginger and honey add a delightful flavor without significantly increasing the GI. It's a healthy and tasty choice for a side dish.

Roasted Rosemary and Garlic Sweet Potatoes

- Difficulty Level: ☐☐
- Preparation Time: 15 minutes
- Cooking Time: 25-30 minutes
- Cooking Skill: Easy

Ingredients for Two:

- 2 large sweet potatoes, peeled and cut into chunks or wedges
- 2 tablespoons olive oil
- 2-3 cloves garlic, minced
- 1-2 sprigs of fresh rosemary, leaves removed and finely chopped
- Salt and black pepper to taste

Instructions:

1. Preheat the Oven:

2. Preheat your oven to 425°F (220°C).

3. Prepare the Sweet Potatoes:

4. Peel the sweet potatoes and cut them into chunks or wedges, depending on your preference. Make sure they are of a similar size for even cooking.

5. *Make the Garlic and Rosemary Oil:*

6. *In a small bowl, mix together the olive oil, minced garlic, and chopped fresh rosemary.*

7. *Coat the Sweet Potatoes:*

8. *Place the sweet potato pieces in a large mixing bowl. Drizzle the garlic and rosemary oil mixture over the sweet potatoes. Toss them to ensure even coating. Season with salt and black pepper to taste.*

9. *Roast:*

10. *Transfer the sweet potatoes to a baking sheet or roasting pan. Spread them out in a single layer. Roast in the preheated oven for 25-30 minutes or until they are tender, turning them occasionally for even browning.*

11. *Serve:*

12. *Remove the roasted sweet potatoes from the oven when they are golden brown and tender. You can garnish them with a few extra fresh rosemary leaves before serving.*

13. *Enjoy:*

14. *Serve your roasted sweet potatoes with rosemary and garlic as a delightful side dish. They are a perfect blend of sweet and savory, making a wonderful accompaniment to various main courses.*

Nutritional Information (per serving):

Calories: Approximately 150-200 (may vary based on portion sizes)

Protein: 2-3g

Fat: 7-10g

Carbohydrates: 25-30g

Fiber: 4-5g

Sugars: 6-8g

Glycemic Index (GI): Sweet potatoes are considered a medium GI food, but roasting them in this way can help maintain a moderate GI for this dish. The garlic and rosemary add great flavor without significantly affecting the GI. It's a nutritious and tasty choice for a side dish.

Roasted Broccoli with Cheese and Lemon

- *Difficulty Level:* ☐☐
- *Preparation Time: 10 minutes*
- *Cooking Time: 20-25 minutes*
- *Cooking Skill: Easy*

Ingredients for Two:

- *2 cups of fresh broccoli florets*
- *1-2 tablespoons olive oil*
- *1/4 cup grated Parmesan or your choice of cheese*
- *1 lemon, zest and juice*
- *Salt and black pepper to taste*

Instructions:

1. *Preheat the Oven:*

2. *Preheat your oven to 425°F (220°C).*

3. *Prepare the Broccoli:*

4. Wash the fresh broccoli florets and pat them dry with a kitchen towel.

5. Toss with Olive Oil:

6. In a large mixing bowl, toss the broccoli florets with 1-2 tablespoons of olive oil to ensure they are evenly coated.

7. Season:

8. Season the broccoli with a pinch of salt and black pepper. Add the lemon zest and give it a good toss to distribute the flavors.

9. Roast:

10. Spread the seasoned broccoli out on a baking sheet in a single layer. Roast in the preheated oven for 20-25 minutes or until the edges are crispy and they are tender when pierced with a fork.

11. Add Cheese:

12. About 5 minutes before the broccoli is done roasting, sprinkle the grated Parmesan cheese over the top. Return the broccoli to the oven for the cheese to melt and become slightly golden.

13. Serve:

14. Remove the roasted broccoli from the oven. Drizzle the lemon juice over the top and give it one last toss.

15. Enjoy:

16. Serve your roasted broccoli with cheese and lemon as a delicious and nutritious side dish. It's a perfect combination of savory and zesty flavors.

Nutritional Information (per serving):

Calories: Approximately 70-90 (may vary based on portion sizes)

Protein: 3-5g

Fat: 5-7g

Carbohydrates: 4-6g

Fiber: 2-3g

Sugars: 2-3g

Glycemic Index (GI): Broccoli is a low GI vegetable, and roasting it in this manner maintains its low GI value. The lemon adds a burst of freshness without affecting the GI significantly. This side dish is both delicious and healthy.

Roasted Cauliflower with Bread Crumbs

- Difficulty Level: ☐☐
- Preparation Time: 10 minutes
- Cooking Time: 30-35 minutes
- Cooking Skill: Easy

Ingredients for Two:

- 1 head of cauliflower, cut into florets
- 2-3 tablespoons olive oil
- 1/4 cup bread crumbs
- 2 cloves garlic, minced
- 1/4 cup grated Parmesan cheese
- 1 tablespoon fresh parsley, chopped
- Salt and black pepper to taste

Instructions:

1. Preheat the Oven:

2. Preheat your oven to 400°F (200°C).

3. Prepare the Cauliflower:

4. Cut the head of cauliflower into florets. Wash them and allow them to drain.

5. Toss with Olive Oil:

6. In a large mixing bowl, toss the cauliflower florets with 2-3 tablespoons of olive oil to coat them evenly.

7. Season:

8. Season the cauliflower with a pinch of salt and black pepper. Toss to distribute the seasoning.

9. Roast:

10. Spread the seasoned cauliflower out on a baking sheet in a single layer. Roast in the preheated oven for 30-35 minutes, or until the cauliflower is tender and lightly browned.

11. Prepare the Bread Crumb Mixture:

12. While the cauliflower is roasting, prepare the bread crumb mixture. In a small skillet, heat a little olive oil over medium heat. Add minced garlic and sauté for a minute. Add the bread crumbs and continue to sauté until they become golden brown.

13. Add Cheese and Parsley:

14. Remove the skillet from heat and stir in the grated Parmesan cheese and chopped fresh parsley.

15. Coat the Cauliflower:

16. When the cauliflower is done roasting, transfer it to a serving dish. Sprinkle the bread crumb mixture over the top, coating the cauliflower evenly.

Nutritional Information (per serving):

Calories: Approximately 100-120 (may vary based on portion sizes)

Protein: 4-6g

Fat: 7-9g

Carbohydrates: 8-10g

Fiber: 3-4g

Sugars: 2-3g

Glycemic Index (GI): Cauliflower has a low GI value, and roasting it in this manner maintains its low GI. The bread crumbs and Parmesan cheese add a satisfying crunch without significantly affecting the GI. This side dish is a delightful addition to your meal.

Stuffed Bell Peppers with Brown Rice and Tomatoes

- Difficulty Level: ☐☐
- Preparation Time: 20 minutes
- Cooking Time: 50-60 minutes
- Cooking Skill: Intermediate

Ingredients for Two:

- 2 large bell peppers, any color
- 1 cup brown rice, cooked
- 1 cup diced tomatoes
- 1/2 cup black beans, cooked (canned or homemade)
- 1/2 cup corn kernels (fresh, frozen, or canned)
- 1/4 cup diced onion
- 1/4 cup diced green bell pepper
- 1/4 cup shredded cheddar cheese (optional)
- 1/2 teaspoon chili powder
- Salt and black pepper to taste
- Olive oil for drizzling

Instructions:

1. *Preheat the Oven:*

2. *Preheat your oven to 350°F (175°C).*

3. *Prepare the Bell Peppers:*

4. *Cut the tops off the bell peppers, remove the seeds and membranes. Rinse them and set aside.*

5. *Cook the Rice:*

6. *Cook the brown rice according to package instructions. You can use a rice cooker or stovetop method.*

7. *Prepare the Filling:*

8. *In a large mixing bowl, combine the cooked brown rice, diced tomatoes, black beans, corn, diced onion, diced green bell pepper, chili powder, salt, and black pepper. Mix everything together until well combined.*

9. *Stuff the Peppers:*

10. *Stuff each bell pepper with the rice and vegetable mixture. Press the mixture down gently as you fill each pepper. If you'd like to add cheese, sprinkle it on top of the filling in each pepper.*

11. *Place in Baking Dish:*

12. *Drizzle a small amount of olive oil in the bottom of a baking dish. Place the stuffed bell peppers upright in the dish.*

13. *Cover and Bake:*

14. *Cover the baking dish with aluminum foil and bake in the preheated oven for 45-50 minutes. The peppers should become tender.*

15. *Remove the Foil:*

16. *Remove the foil and bake for an additional 5-10 minutes, or until the cheese (if used) is melted and the tops of the peppers have a slight browning.*

17. *Serve:*

18. *Carefully remove the stuffed bell peppers from the oven. Let them cool for a few minutes before serving.*

19. *Enjoy:*

20. *Serve your stuffed bell peppers with brown rice and tomatoes as a wholesome and satisfying meal.*

Nutritional Information (per serving):

Calories: Approximately 350-400 (may vary based on portion sizes)
Protein: 10-12g
Fat: 5-7g
Carbohydrates: 70-80g
Fiber: 8-10g
Sugars: 5-7g

Glycemic Index (GI): The overall GI for this dish is moderate to low, mainly due to the presence of brown rice. However, the fiber from the brown rice and vegetables helps stabilize blood sugar levels.

Stuffed Mushrooms with Spinach and Cheese

- *Difficulty Level: ☐☐*
- *Preparation Time: 20 minutes*
- *Cooking Time: 25 minutes*
- *Cooking Skill: Intermediate*

Ingredients for Two:

- *8-10 large white mushrooms*
- *1 cup fresh spinach, chopped*
- *1/2 cup cream cheese*
- *1/4 cup grated Parmesan cheese*
- *2 cloves garlic, minced*
- *2 tablespoons breadcrumbs*
- *2 tablespoons olive oil*
- *Salt and black pepper to taste*
- *Fresh parsley, for garnish (optional)*

Instructions:

1. *Preheat the Oven:*

2. *Preheat your oven to 350°F (175°C).*

3. *Prepare the Mushrooms:*

4. *Gently wipe the mushrooms clean with a damp cloth. Carefully remove the stems, creating a hollow space for the filling.*

5. *Prepare the Filling:*

6. *In a skillet, heat 1 tablespoon of olive oil over medium heat. Add minced garlic and chopped spinach. Sauté for 2-3 minutes until the spinach wilts. Remove from heat.*

7. *Prepare the Cheese Mixture:*

8. *In a mixing bowl, combine cream cheese, grated Parmesan cheese, sautéed spinach, breadcrumbs, salt, and black pepper. Mix until well combined.*

9. *Stuff the Mushrooms:*

10. *Using a spoon or your hands, stuff each mushroom cap with the cheese and spinach mixture. Press down gently to ensure they are well filled.*

11. *Drizzle with Olive Oil:*

12. *Place the stuffed mushrooms on a baking sheet. Drizzle them with the remaining 1 tablespoon of olive oil.*

13. *Bake:*

14. *Place the baking sheet in the preheated oven and bake for about 20-25 minutes,*

or until the mushrooms are tender and the tops are golden brown.

15. *Garnish and Serve:*

16. *Optionally, garnish with fresh parsley before serving. Arrange the stuffed mushrooms on a serving platter and enjoy!*

Nutritional Information (per serving):

Calories: Approximately 250-300 (may vary based on portion sizes)

Protein: 6-8g

Fat: 18-20g

Carbohydrates: 10-12g

Fiber: 2-3g

Sugars: 2-3g

Glycemic Index (GI): The overall GI for this dish is low, as mushrooms have a low GI, and the filling doesn't contain high-GI ingredients.

SALADS

Quinoa Salad with Chickpeas and Cherry Tomatoes

- *Difficulty Level:* □
- *Preparation Time: 15 minutes*
- *Cooking Skill: Easy*
- *Servings: 2*

Ingredients:

- *1 cup quinoa*
- *1 can (15 oz) chickpeas, drained and rinsed*

- *1 cup cherry tomatoes, halved*
- *1/4 cup red onion, finely chopped*
- *1/4 cup fresh parsley, chopped*
- *2 tablespoons extra-virgin olive oil*
- *1 tablespoon lemon juice*
- *Salt and black pepper, to taste*

Instructions:

1. *Cook the Quinoa:*

2. *Rinse the quinoa under cold water to remove any bitterness. In a saucepan, combine the rinsed quinoa with 2 cups of water. Bring it to a boil, then reduce the heat to low, cover, and simmer for about 15 minutes or until the quinoa is cooked and the water is absorbed. Remove from heat, fluff with a fork, and let it cool.*

3. *Prepare the Salad:*

4. *In a large mixing bowl, combine the cooked quinoa, chickpeas, halved cherry tomatoes, finely chopped red onion, and fresh parsley.*

5. *Make the Dressing:*

6. *In a small bowl, whisk together the extra-virgin olive oil, lemon juice, salt, and black pepper.*

7. *Combine and Toss:*

8. *Pour the dressing over the salad ingredients. Toss everything together until well combined and evenly coated with the dressing.*

9. Serve:

10. Divide the quinoa salad into two servings and enjoy!

Nutritional Information (per serving):

Calories: Approximately 400-450

Protein: 14-16g

Fat: 14-16g

Carbohydrates: 58-62g

Fiber: 10-12g

Sugars: 7-9g

Glycemic Index (GI): The overall GI of this dish is moderate, as quinoa has a moderate GI and the presence of chickpeas and vegetables may affect the GI slightly. It's a healthy and balanced option for your meal.

Greek Salad with Cucumbers, Tomatoes, and Feta:

- Difficulty Level: ☐☐
- Preparation Time: 15 minutes
- Cooking Skill: Easy
- Servings: 2

Ingredients:

- 2 cucumbers, diced
- 2 medium tomatoes, diced
- 1/2 red onion, thinly sliced
- 1/2 cup feta cheese, diced
- Black olives, as desired
- Dried oregano, to taste
- Extra virgin olive oil
- Lemon juice
- Salt and pepper, to taste

Instructions:

1. In a large bowl, combine cucumbers, tomatoes, red onion, and feta.
2. Add black olives and a sprinkle of dried oregano.
3. Dress the salad with extra virgin olive oil, lemon juice, salt, and pepper to taste.
4. Mix well and serve.

Nutritional Values (per serving):

Calories: About 250-300

Protein: About 8-10g

Fat: About 18-20g

Carbohydrates: About 15-20g

Fiber: About 4-6g

Sugars: About 8-10g

Spinach Salad with Strawberries and Walnuts:

- Difficulty Level: ☐☐
- Preparation Time: 10 minutes
- Cooking Skill: Easy
- Servings: 2

Ingredients:

- 4 cups fresh spinach
- 1 cup strawberries, sliced
- 1/4 cup walnuts, toasted and chopped
- Goat cheese, as desired
- Balsamic or vinaigrette dressing, as desired

Instructions:

1. In a large bowl, combine fresh spinach, strawberries, and walnuts.
2. Add diced goat cheese if desired.
3. Dress the salad with balsamic or a light vinaigrette dressing, as desired.
4. Mix well and serve.

Nutritional Values (per serving):

Calories: About 200-250

Protein: About 6-8g

Fat: About 12-15g

Carbohydrates: About 15-20g

Fiber: About 4-6g

Sugars: About 8-10g

Red Cabbage Salad with Apple and Walnuts:

- *Difficulty Level:* ☐☐
- *Preparation Time: 15 minutes*
- *Cooking Skill: Easy*
- *Servings: 2*

Ingredients:

- *4 cups red cabbage, finely sliced*
- *1 green apple, diced*
- *1/4 cup walnuts, toasted and chopped*
- *2 tablespoons light mayonnaise*
- *1 tablespoon apple cider vinegar*
- *Honey, to taste (optional)*
- *Salt and pepper, to taste*

Instructions:

1. In a large bowl, combine red cabbage, green apple, and walnuts.
2. In a small container, mix light mayonnaise and apple cider vinegar. Add a bit of honey if you desire a touch of sweetness.

3. Dress the salad with the prepared dressing and mix well.
4. Season with salt and pepper to taste.
5. Serve the red cabbage salad with apple and walnuts.

Nutritional Values (per serving):

Calories: About 200-250

Protein: About 2-3g

Fat: About 10-12g

Carbohydrates: About 30-35g

Fiber: About 6-8g

Sugars: About 20-25g

Here are the translations into American English for the remaining salad recipes:

Cucumber Salad with Yogurt and Dill Dressing:

- *Difficulty Level:* ☐☐
- *Preparation Time: 10 minutes*
- *Cooking Skill: Easy*
- *Servings: 2*

Ingredients:

- *2 cucumbers, thinly sliced*
- *1/2 cup Greek yogurt*
- *2 tablespoons fresh dill, chopped*
- *1 garlic clove, minced*
- *Lemon juice, to taste*
- *Salt and pepper, to taste*

Instructions:

1. In a bowl, combine thinly sliced cucumbers.

2. In a separate bowl, mix Greek yogurt, fresh dill, minced garlic, lemon juice, salt, and pepper to create the dressing.
3. Pour the dressing over the cucumbers and toss to coat.
4. Serve the cucumber salad with yogurt and dill dressing.

Nutritional Values (per serving):

Calories: About 70-90
Protein: About 5-6g
Fat: About 2-3g
Carbohydrates: About 8-10g
Fiber: About 1-2g
Sugars: About 5-6g

Lentil Salad with Bell Peppers and Olives:

- Difficulty Level: ☐☐
- Preparation Time: 20 minutes
- Cooking Skill: Easy
- Servings: 2

Ingredients:

- 1 cup cooked green or brown lentils
- 1 red bell pepper, diced
- 1 yellow bell pepper, diced
- Black or green olives, to taste
- Red wine vinegar, to taste
- Extra virgin olive oil, to taste
- Salt and pepper, to taste

Instructions:

1. In a bowl, combine cooked lentils, diced red and yellow bell peppers, and olives.
2. Dress the salad with red wine vinegar, extra virgin olive oil, salt, and pepper to taste.

3. Mix well and serve the lentil salad with bell peppers and olives.

Nutritional Values (per serving):

Calories: About 250-300
Protein: About 10-12g
Fat: About 8-10g
Carbohydrates: About 40-45g
Fiber: About 12-15g
Sugars: About 4-6g

Arugula Salad with Pears and Goat Cheese:

- Difficulty Level: ☐☐
- Preparation Time: 15 minutes
- Cooking Skill: Easy
- Servings: 2

Ingredients:

- 4 cups fresh arugula
- 2 ripe pears, thinly sliced
- 1/2 cup crumbled goat cheese
- Pecans or walnuts, to taste
- Balsamic vinaigrette dressing, as desired

Instructions:

1. In a large bowl, combine fresh arugula, thinly sliced pears, crumbled goat cheese, and pecans or walnuts.
2. Dress the salad with balsamic vinaigrette dressing as desired.
3. Mix well and serve the arugula salad with pears and goat cheese.

Nutritional Values (per serving):

Calories: About 250-300

Protein: About 6-8g

Fat: About 12-15g

Carbohydrates: About 30-35g

Fiber: About 6-8g

Sugars: About 18-20g

Chickpea Salad with Parsley and Red Onion:

- Difficulty Level: ☐☐
- Preparation Time: 15 minutes
- Cooking Skill: Easy
- Servings: 2

Ingredients:

- 1 can (15 oz) chickpeas, drained and rinsed
- Fresh parsley, chopped
- 1/4 red onion, finely sliced
- Lemon juice, to taste
- Extra virgin olive oil, to taste
- Salt and pepper, to taste

Instructions:

1. In a bowl, combine chickpeas, fresh parsley, and finely sliced red onion.
2. Drizzle with lemon juice, extra virgin olive oil, and season with salt and pepper.
3. Mix well and serve the chickpea salad with parsley and red onion.

Nutritional Values (per serving):

Calories: About 250-300

Protein: About 10-12g

Fat: About 12-15g

Carbohydrates: About 30-35g

Fiber: About 8-10g

Sugars: About 6-8g

Potato Salad with Mustard and Cucumbers:

- Difficulty Level: ☐☐
- Preparation Time: 20 minutes
- Cooking Skill: Easy
- Servings: 2

Ingredients:

- 4 cups cooked and diced potatoes
- Cucumbers, diced
- Dijon mustard, to taste
- Red wine vinegar, to taste
- Extra virgin olive oil, to taste

Salt and pepper, to taste

Instructions:

1. In a large bowl, combine diced potatoes and diced cucumbers.
2. Dress the salad with Dijon mustard, red wine vinegar, extra virgin olive oil, salt, and pepper to taste.
3. Mix well and serve the potato salad with mustard and cucumbers.

Nutritional Values (per serving):

Calories: About 250-300

Protein: About 6-8g

Fat: About 8-10g

Carbohydrates: About 35-40g

Fiber: About 5-7g

Sugars: About 4-6g

Quinoa Salad with Avocado and Corn:

- *Difficulty Level:* ☐☐
- *Preparation Time: 15 minutes*
- *Cooking Skill: Easy*
- *Servings: 2*

Ingredients:

- *1 cup cooked quinoa*
- *Avocado, diced*
- *Corn kernels*
- *Fresh cilantro, chopped*
- *Lime juice, to taste*
- *Salt and pepper, to taste*

Instructions:

1. *In a bowl, combine cooked quinoa, diced avocado, corn kernels, and chopped fresh cilantro.*
2. *Drizzle with lime juice, and season with salt and pepper.*
3. *Mix well and serve the quinoa salad with avocado and corn.*

Nutritional Values (per serving):

Calories: About 300-350

Protein: About 6-8g

Fat: About 10-12g

Carbohydrates: About 40-45g

Fiber: About 6-8g

Sugars: About 3-4g

PUREE & PESTO

Mashed Sweet Potatoes with Cinnamon:

- *Difficulty Level:* ☐

- *Preparation Time: 30 minutes*
- *Cooking Skill: Easy*
- *Servings: 2*

Ingredients:

- *2 large sweet potatoes, peeled and diced*
- *2-3 tablespoons butter or margarine*
- *1/2 teaspoon ground cinnamon*
- *Salt and pepper, to taste*

Instructions:

1. *Boil or steam the sweet potato pieces until they are tender, about 20-25 minutes.*
2. *Drain and mash the sweet potatoes with butter, ground cinnamon, salt, and pepper until smooth.*
3. *Serve the mashed sweet potatoes with a sprinkle of extra cinnamon if desired.*

Nutritional Values (per serving):

Calories: About 200-250

Protein: About 2-3g

Fat: About 7-9g

Carbohydrates: About 35-40g

Fiber: About 6-8g

Sugars: About 7-9g

Cauliflower Mash with Garlic and Parsley:

- *Difficulty Level:* ☐
- *Preparation Time: 25 minutes*
- *Cooking Skill: Easy*
- *Servings: 2*

Ingredients:

- 1 head of cauliflower, cut into florets
- 2-3 cloves garlic, minced
- 2-3 tablespoons butter or margarine
- Fresh parsley, chopped
- Salt and pepper, to taste

Instructions:

1. Steam or boil the cauliflower florets until they are very tender, about 15-20 minutes.
2. Drain and mash the cauliflower with minced garlic, butter, salt, and pepper until it reaches your desired consistency.
3. Garnish with chopped fresh parsley.

Nutritional Values (per serving):

Calories: About 100-150

Protein: About 3-4g

Fat: About 7-9g

Carbohydrates: About 10-15g

Fiber: About 5-6g

Sugars: About 3-4g

Carrot Puree with Cumin:

- Difficulty Level: ☐
- Preparation Time: 20 minutes
- Cooking Skill: Easy
- Servings: 2

Ingredients:

- 4-5 large carrots, peeled and sliced
- 2-3 tablespoons butter or margarine
- 1/2 teaspoon ground cumin
- Salt and pepper, to taste

Instructions:

1. Steam or boil the carrot slices until they are very soft, about 15-20 minutes.
2. Drain and mash the carrots with butter, ground cumin, salt, and pepper until smooth.
3. Serve the carrot puree with a sprinkle of extra cumin if desired.

Nutritional Values (per serving):

Calories: About 150-200

Protein: About 2-3g

Fat: About 7-9g

Carbohydrates: About 20-25g

Fiber: About 5-6g

Sugars: About 8-10g

Basil Pesto with Walnuts and Parmesan:

- Difficulty Level: ☐
- Preparation Time: 15 minutes
- Cooking Skill: Easy
- Servings: 4

Ingredients:

- 2 cups fresh basil leaves
- 1/2 cup walnuts
- 1/2 cup grated Parmesan cheese
- 2 cloves garlic
- 1/2 cup extra-virgin olive oil
- Salt and pepper, to taste

Instructions:

1. In a food processor, combine the basil, walnuts, Parmesan cheese, and garlic. Pulse until finely chopped.

2. With the food processor running, slowly drizzle in the olive oil until the pesto reaches your desired consistency.
3. Season with salt and pepper to taste.
4. Serve the basil pesto with pasta or as a spread.

Arugula Pesto with Pine Nuts and Pecorino:

- *Difficulty Level: ☐*
- *Preparation Time: 15 minutes*
- *Cooking Skill: Easy*
- *Servings: 4*

Ingredients:

- *2 cups fresh arugula*
- *1/2 cup pine nuts*
- *1/2 cup grated Pecorino cheese*
- *2 cloves garlic*
- *1/2 cup extra-virgin olive oil*
- *Salt and pepper, to taste*

Instructions:

1. In a food processor, combine the arugula, pine nuts, Pecorino cheese, and garlic. Pulse until finely chopped.
2. With the food processor running, slowly drizzle in the olive oil until the pesto reaches your desired consistency.
3. Season with salt and pepper to taste.
4. Serve the arugula pesto with pasta or as a spread.

Cumin-Spiced Hummus:

- *Difficulty Level: ☐*
- *Preparation Time: 10 minutes*
- *Cooking Skill: Easy*
- *Servings: 4*

Ingredients:

- *2 cups canned chickpeas, drained and rinsed*
- *1/4 cup tahini*
- *2 cloves garlic*
- *2 tablespoons lemon juice*
- *1 teaspoon ground cumin*
- *1/2 teaspoon smoked paprika*
- *1/4 cup extra-virgin olive oil*
- *Salt and pepper, to taste*

Instructions:

1. In a food processor, combine the chickpeas, tahini, garlic, lemon juice, cumin, and smoked paprika. Process until smooth.
2. With the food processor running, slowly drizzle in the olive oil until the hummus reaches your desired consistency.
3. Season with salt and pepper to taste.
4. Serve the cumin-spiced hummus with pita bread, veggies, or as a dip.

Zucchini Pesto with Basil and Almonds:

- *Difficulty Level: ☐*
- *Preparation Time: 15 minutes*
- *Cooking Skill: Easy*
- *Servings: 4*

Ingredients:

- *2 cups chopped zucchini*
- *1 cup fresh basil leaves*
- *1/4 cup almonds*
- *2 cloves garlic*
- *1/2 cup extra-virgin olive oil*
- *Salt and pepper, to taste*

Instructions:

1. In a food processor, combine the zucchini, basil, almonds, and garlic. Pulse until finely chopped.
2. With the food processor running, slowly drizzle in the olive oil until the pesto reaches your desired consistency.
3. Season with salt and pepper to taste.
4. Serve the zucchini pesto with pasta or as a spread.

Beet Hummus with Herbs:

- Difficulty Level: □
- Preparation Time: 10 minutes
- Cooking Skill: Easy
- Servings: 4

Ingredients:

- 2 cups canned chickpeas, drained and rinsed
- 1/2 cup roasted beets, diced
- 1/4 cup fresh herbs (e.g., parsley, cilantro, dill)
- 2 cloves garlic
- 2 tablespoons lemon juice
- 1/4 cup extra-virgin olive oil
- Salt and pepper, to taste

Instructions:

1. In a food processor, combine the chickpeas, beets, herbs, garlic, and lemon juice. Process until smooth.
2. With the food processor running, slowly drizzle in the olive oil until the hummus reaches your desired consistency.
3. Season with salt and pepper to taste.
4. Serve the beet hummus with pita bread, veggies, or as a dip.

Butternut Squash Puree with Nutmeg:

- Difficulty Level: □
- Preparation Time: 30 minutes
- Cooking Skill: Easy
- Servings: 4

Ingredients:

- 2 cups butternut squash, cubed
- 1/4 cup butter
- 1/4 teaspoon ground nutmeg
- Salt and pepper, to taste

Instructions:

1. Steam or boil the butternut squash until tender. Drain well.
2. In a blender or food processor, combine the cooked butternut squash, butter, nutmeg, salt, and pepper. Blend until smooth.
3. Serve the butternut squash puree as a side dish.

Parsley Pesto with Walnuts and Lemon:

- Difficulty Level: □
- Preparation Time: 15 minutes
- Cooking Skill: Easy
- Servings: 4

Ingredients:

- 2 cups fresh parsley leaves
- 1/2 cup walnuts
- 1/2 cup grated lemon zest
- 2 cloves garlic
- 1/2 cup extra-virgin olive oil
- Salt and pepper, to taste

Instructions:

1. In a food processor, combine the parsley, walnuts, lemon zest, and garlic. Pulse until finely chopped.
2. With the food processor running, slowly drizzle in the olive oil until the pesto reaches your desired consistency.
3. Season with salt and pepper to taste.
4. Serve the parsley pesto with pasta or as a spread.

SAUSES & PICKLES

Pickled Cucumbers in Apple Cider Vinegar:

- Difficulty Level: ☐
- Preparation Time: 20 minutes
- Cooking Skill: Easy
- Servings: 4

Ingredients:

- 2 cups sliced cucumbers
- 1 cup apple cider vinegar
- 1/4 cup sugar
- 1 teaspoon salt
- 1/2 teaspoon black peppercorns
- 1/2 teaspoon dill seeds (optional)

Instructions:

1. In a saucepan, combine the apple cider vinegar, sugar, salt, peppercorns, and dill seeds (if using). Heat over medium heat until the sugar and salt dissolve.
2. Place the sliced cucumbers in a glass jar or container.
3. Pour the vinegar mixture over the cucumbers, ensuring they are completely covered.

4. Allow the pickles to cool, then cover and refrigerate for at least 24 hours before serving.

Pickled Carrots with Ginger and Coriander:

- Difficulty Level: ☐
- Preparation Time: 20 minutes
- Cooking Skill: Easy
- Servings: 4

Ingredients:

- 2 cups sliced carrots
- 1 cup rice vinegar
- 1/4 cup sugar
- 1 teaspoon salt
- 2 tablespoons fresh ginger, sliced
- 1 teaspoon coriander seeds

Instructions:

1. In a saucepan, combine the rice vinegar, sugar, salt, ginger, and coriander seeds. Heat over medium heat until the sugar and salt dissolve.
2. Place the sliced carrots in a glass jar or container.
3. Pour the vinegar mixture over the carrots, ensuring they are completely covered.
4. Allow the pickles to cool, then cover and refrigerate for at least 24 hours before serving.

Herbed Yogurt Sauce:

- Difficulty Level: ☐
- Preparation Time: 10 minutes
- Cooking Skill: Easy
- Servings: 4

Ingredients:

1. 1 cup plain yogurt
2. 2 tablespoons fresh herbs
   (e.g., mint, dill, chives), finely chopped
3. 1 clove garlic, minced
4. 1 tablespoon lemon juice
5. Salt and pepper, to taste

Instructions:

1. In a bowl, combine the plain yogurt,
   fresh herbs, minced garlic,
   and lemon juice. Mix well.
2. Season with salt and pepper to taste.
3. Serve the herbed yogurt sauce as a dip
   or condiment.
4.

Tahini Sauce with Garlic and Lemon:

- Difficulty Level: ☐
- Preparation Time: 10 minutes
- Cooking Skill: Easy
- Servings: 4

Ingredients:

- 1/2 cup tahini
- 1 clove garlic, minced
- 2 tablespoons lemon juice
- 2 tablespoons water (or more for
  desired consistency)
- Salt, to taste

Instructions:

1. In a bowl, combine the tahini, minced
   garlic, lemon juice, and water. Mix until
   smooth.
2. Add more water if needed to achieve
   your desired sauce consistency.
3. Season with salt to taste.

4. Serve the tahini sauce as a dip or
   drizzle it over dishes.

Avocado Sauce with Lime and Black Pepper:

- Difficulty Level: ☐
- Preparation Time: 10 minutes
- Cooking Skill: Easy
- Servings: 4

Ingredients:

- 2 ripe avocados
- Juice of 2 limes
- 1/2 teaspoon black pepper
- Salt, to taste

Instructions:

1. Scoop the flesh of the avocados into a
   bowl and mash it with a fork until
   smooth.
2. Add the lime juice, black pepper,
   and salt. Mix well.
3. Serve the avocado sauce as a
   dip or drizzle it over dishes.

Guacamole with Tomato and Red Onion:

1. Difficulty Level: ☐
2. Preparation Time: 15 minutes
3. Cooking Skill: Easy
4. Servings: 4

Ingredients:

- 2 ripe avocados
- 2 tomatoes, diced
- 1/2 red onion, finely chopped
- Juice of 1 lime
- 2 tablespoons fresh cilantro,

chopped
- *Salt and black pepper, to taste*

Instructions:

1. *Scoop the flesh of the avocados into a bowl and mash it with a fork until slightly chunky.*
2. *Add the diced tomatoes, chopped red onion, lime juice, and cilantro. Mix well.*
3. *Season with salt and black pepper to taste.*
4. *Serve the guacamole with tortilla chips or as a topping for various dishes.*
5.

Curry Sauce with Greek Yogurt:

- *Difficulty Level: ☐☐*
- *Preparation Time: 20 minutes*
- *Cooking Skill: Intermediate*
- *Servings: 4*

Ingredients:

- *1 cup Greek yogurt*
- *2 tablespoons curry powder*
- *2 cloves garlic, minced*
- *2 tablespoons olive oil*
- *Salt and pepper, to taste*

Instructions:

1. *In a bowl, combine the Greek yogurt, curry powder, minced garlic, and olive oil. Mix until the sauce is well blended.*
2. *Season with salt and pepper to taste.*
3. *This curry sauce is a delightful accompaniment for various dishes.*

Greek Yogurt Sauce with Cucumbers and Garlic:

- *Difficulty Level: ☐*
- *Preparation Time: 10 minutes*
- *Cooking Skill: Easy*
- *Servings: 4*

Ingredients:

- *1 cup Greek yogurt*
- *1 cucumber, finely grated*
- *2 cloves garlic, minced*
- *1 tablespoon fresh dill, chopped*
- *Juice of 1 lemon*
- *Salt and black pepper, to taste*

Instructions:

1. *In a bowl, combine the Greek yogurt, grated cucumber, minced garlic, chopped dill, and lemon juice. Mix well.*
2. *Season with salt and black pepper to taste.*
3. *Serve the Greek yogurt sauce as a dip or condiment.*

Homemade Barbecue Sauce:

- *Difficulty Level: ☐☐*
- *Preparation Time: 30 minutes*
- *Cooking Skill: Intermediate*
- *Servings: 4*

Ingredients:

- *1 cup ketchup*
- *1/4 cup brown sugar*
- *2 tablespoons molasses*
- *2 tablespoons apple cider vinegar*

- *1 tablespoon Worcestershire sauce*
- *1 teaspoon smoked paprika*
- *1/2 teaspoon garlic powder*
- *1/2 teaspoon onion powder*
- *1/4 teaspoon cayenne peppe
r (adjust to taste)*
- *Salt and black pepper, to taste*

Instructions:

1. *In a saucepan, combine the ketchup, brown sugar, molasses, apple cider vinegar, Worcestershire sauce, smoked paprika, garlic powder, onion powder, and cayenne pepper.*
2. *Cook over low heat, stirring occasionally, for about 20-30 minutes, or until the sauce thickens.*
3. *Season with salt and black pepper to taste.*
4. *Allow the barbecue sauce to cool before using it for grilling or as a condiment.*

DESSERTS

Fruit Skewers with Dark Chocolate

- *Difficulty Level: □□*
- *Preparation Time: 20 minutes*
- *Servings: 4*

Ingredients:

- *Assorted fresh fruits (e.g., strawberries, pineapple, banana, kiwi, and apple), cut into bite-sized pieces*
- *4 ounces dark chocolate, chopped*
- *2 tablespoons coconut oil*
- *Wooden skewers*

Instructions:

Start by preparing the fresh fruits. Wash and peel if necessary, then cut them into bite-sized pieces.

Thread the fruit pieces onto wooden skewers, creating colorful and varied combinations on each skewer. Leave some space at the ends for easier handling.

In a microwave-safe bowl, combine the chopped dark chocolate and coconut oil.

Microwave the chocolate and coconut oil in 20-30 second intervals, stirring in between until the chocolate is completely melted and the mixture is smooth.

Drizzle the melted chocolate over the fruit skewers or dip the fruit skewers into the chocolate, coating them generously.

Place the chocolate-covered fruit skewers on a baking sheet lined with parchment paper. This will help prevent them from sticking.

Allow the chocolate to set. You can speed up the process by placing the fruit skewers in the refrigerator for about 10-15 minutes.

Once the chocolate has hardened, your Fruit Skewers with Dark Chocolate are ready to serve.

Nutritional Information (per serving):

Calories: 160

Fat: 8g

Carbohydrates: 20g

Fiber: 3g

Sugar: 13g

Protein: 2g

Banana Ice Cream with Walnut Crumble:

Difficulty: ☐☐
Prep Time: 10 minutes
Freezing Time: 4-6 hours
Servings: 2

Ingredients:

2 ripe bananas, peeled, sliced, and frozen
1/2 teaspoon lemon juice
1/4 teaspoon vanilla extract (optional)
1/4 cup coarsely chopped walnuts

Instructions:

Start by slicing the ripe bananas into rounds and placing them in an airtight bag. Ensure they are very ripe, as this will give the ice cream a naturally sweet flavor.

Freeze the banana slices for at least 4-6 hours or until completely frozen.

Once the banana slices are completely frozen, place them in a powerful blender along with lemon juice and vanilla extract, if desired. The vanilla extract will add a pleasant aromatic note to the ice cream, but it's optional.

Blend the ingredients until you achieve a creamy and smooth consistency. You may need to scrape the sides of the blender occasionally to ensure everything is well mixed.

Pour the banana ice cream into a bowl and gently fold in the coarsely chopped walnuts.

Transfer the Banana Ice Cream with Walnut Crumble to an airtight container and place it in the freezer for an additional hour if you want a firmer consistency, or serve immediately for a softer texture.

Before serving, you can garnish the ice cream with additional chopped walnuts or banana slices.

Enjoy your Banana Ice Cream with Walnut Crumble for two!

Nutritional Values (per serving):

Calories: Approximately 180-220 kcal
Protein: Approximately 3-4g
Fat: Approximately 8-10g
Carbohydrates: Approximately 30-35g
Fiber: Approximately 4-5g
Sugars: Approximately 16-18g

Glycemic Index (GI):

Bananas have a moderate glycemic index (GI), which is typically around 51. The GI of this dessert will be influenced by the ripe bananas used. Riper bananas tend to have a higher GI, while less ripe ones have a lower GI.

Keep in mind that these values are approximate and can vary depending on factors like the ripeness of the bananas and the exact quantity of ingredients used. The GI can also vary depending on individual factors.

Coconut and Oat Biscuits

Difficulty: ☐☐
Preparation Time: 20 minutes
Baking Time: 15-18 minutes

Servings: About 20 biscuits

Ingredients:

1 cup rolled oats

1 cup shredded coconut

1 cup all-purpose flour

1/2 cup unsalted butter, softened

1/2 cup granulated sugar

1/4 cup brown sugar

1 egg

1 teaspoon vanilla extract

1/2 teaspoon baking powder

1/4 teaspoon baking soda

A pinch of salt

Instructions:

Preheat your oven to 350°F (175°C) and line a baking sheet with parchment paper.

In a mixing bowl, combine the rolled oats, shredded coconut, all-purpose flour, baking powder, baking soda, and a pinch of salt.

In another bowl, beat together the softened butter, granulated sugar, and brown sugar until it becomes creamy and well combined.

Add the egg and vanilla extract to the sugar-butter mixture and continue to mix until smooth.

Gradually add the dry ingredients to the wet ingredients, stirring until a dough forms. Make sure not to overmix.

Drop tablespoons of dough onto the prepared baking sheet, spacing them about 2 inches apart. You can use the back of a fork to slightly flatten each cookie.

Bake in the preheated oven for 15-18 minutes or until the edges turn golden brown.

Remove from the oven and let the biscuits cool on the baking sheet for a few minutes, then transfer them to a wire rack to cool completely.

Once they're completely cool, enjoy your homemade Coconut and Oat Biscuits.

Nutritional Information (per biscuit, approximate):

Calories: 100-120

Protein: 1-2g

Fat: 6-8g

Carbohydrates: 12-15g

Fiber: 1-2g

Sugars: 6-8g

The Glycemic Index (GI) for Coconut and Oat Biscuits can vary depending on factors like the specific ingredients and the size of the biscuits. However, oats have a low to medium GI, which is good for keeping blood sugar levels stable. The added sugar in the biscuits may increase the overall GI somewhat.

It's essential to note that GI values can fluctuate, and they depend on various factors, so it's always recommended to consult with a nutritionist or healthcare professional for precise GI information tailored to your specific recipe and ingredients.

Whole Wheat Blueberry Muffins

Difficulty Level: ☐☐

Preparation Time: 15 minutes

Cooking Time: 20-25 minutes

Yield: 12 muffins

For two servings of Whole Wheat Blueberry Muffins:

Ingredients:

3/4 cup whole wheat flour

1/4 cup rolled oats

1/4 cup brown sugar

1 teaspoon baking powder

1/4 teaspoon baking soda

1/4 teaspoon salt

1/4 teaspoon ground cinnamon

1/2 cup plain Greek yogurt

2 tablespoons unsweetened applesauce

2 tablespoons milk (you can use regular milk or a milk alternative)

2 tablespoons honey or maple syrup

1 large egg

1/2 teaspoon vanilla extract

3/4 cup fresh blueberries

Instructions:

Preheat your oven to 350°F (175°C). Line or grease a muffin tin with two cups.

In a bowl, combine the whole wheat flour, rolled oats, brown sugar, baking powder, baking soda, salt, and ground cinnamon.

In another bowl, whisk together the Greek yogurt, applesauce, milk, honey (or maple syrup), egg, and vanilla extract.

Pour the wet ingredients into the dry ingredients and mix until just combined. Avoid overmixing; a few lumps are fine.

Gently fold in the fresh blueberries.

Divide the batter evenly between the two muffin cups, filling each about 2/3 full.

Bake in the preheated oven for 20-25 minutes, or until a toothpick inserted into the center of a muffin comes out clean.

Allow the muffins to cool in the pan for a few minutes before transferring them to a wire rack to cool completely.

Nutritional Information (per muffin, based on a 2-muffin yield):

Calories: Approximately 160-180

Protein: About 5g

Fat: About 2-3g

Carbohydrates: Approximately 34-38g

Fiber: Around 3-4g

Sugar: About 14-16g

Certainly, here's the recipe for "Coconut and Oat Cookies" for two people with information on times and difficulty level:

Coconut and Oat Cookies for Two

Difficulty Level: ☐ ☐

Preparation Time: About 15 minutes

Baking Time: Approximately 10-12 minutes

Servings: Makes about 6 cookies

Ingredients:

1/2 cup old-fashioned oats

1/4 cup whole wheat flour

1/4 cup desiccated coconut

1/4 cup coconut sugar (or your choice of sugar)

1/4 teaspoon baking soda

1/8 teaspoon salt

2 tablespoons melted coconut oil (or canola oil)

1/4 large egg (whisked) - approximately 1.5 tablespoons

1/4 teaspoon vanilla extract

2 tablespoons dark chocolate chips (optional)

Instructions:

Preheat your oven to 350°F (175°C) and line a baking sheet with parchment paper.

In a mixing bowl, combine the oats, whole wheat flour, desiccated coconut, coconut sugar, baking soda, and salt.

In another bowl, mix the melted coconut oil, whisked egg, and vanilla extract.

Combine the wet ingredients with the dry ingredients and stir well. If desired, add the dark chocolate chips and mix until they're evenly distributed in the dough.

With moist hands, form small dough balls and place them on the prepared baking sheet. Slightly flatten each dough ball to form cookies.

Bake in the preheated oven for about 10-12 minutes or until the cookies are lightly golden.

Remove the cookies from the oven and allow them to cool on the baking sheet for a few minutes before transferring them to a cooling rack for complete cooling.

Nutritional Information (per cookie, excluding dark chocolate chips):

Calories: Approximately 90-100

Protein: About 1-2g

Fat: About 5-6g

Carbohydrates: About 10-12g

Fiber: About 1-2g

Sugars: About 4-5g

SMOOTHIE

Green Smoothie with Spinach, Banana, and Avocado

Difficulty Level: ☐
Preparation Time: About 5 minutes
Servings: 2

Ingredients:

2 cups fresh spinach leaves

1 ripe banana

1 ripe avocado

1 cup almond milk (or your choice of milk)

1 tablespoon honey or maple syrup (optional, for sweetness)

Ice cubes (optional)

Instructions:

Wash the fresh spinach leaves and place them in a blender.

Peel and slice the banana. Add the banana slices to the blender.

Cut the avocado in half, remove the pit, and scoop out the flesh into the blender.

Pour in the almond milk (or your choice of milk).

If you prefer a sweeter smoothie, you can add honey or maple syrup to taste.

You can also add ice cubes if you want a colder, thicker smoothie.

Blend all the ingredients until smooth and creamy.

Taste the smoothie and adjust the sweetness or thickness by adding more honey, milk, or ice if needed.

Pour the green smoothie into two glasses and serve immediately.

Nutritional Information (per serving, without added sweeteners):

Calories: Approximately 180-200

Protein: About 2-3g

Fat: About 10-12g

Carbohydrates: About 20-25g

Fiber: About 7-8g

Sugars: About 5-6g

Certainly, here's the recipe for a "Coconut Pineapple Ginger Smoothie":

Coconut Pineapple Ginger Smoothie

Difficulty Level: □
Preparation Time: About 5 minutes
Servings: 2

Ingredients:

1 cup coconut milk (canned or from a carton)

1 cup fresh or canned pineapple chunks

1 small piece of fresh ginger (about 1 inch), peeled and sliced

1 ripe banana

1-2 tablespoons honey or maple syrup (optional, for sweetness)

Ice cubes (optional)

Instructions:

Pour the coconut milk into a blender.

Add the fresh or canned pineapple chunks to the blender.

Add the sliced fresh ginger to the blender. Adjust the amount of ginger to your taste; more ginger will make the smoothie spicier.

Peel and slice the ripe banana and add it to the blender.

If you'd like to sweeten the smoothie, you can add honey or maple syrup to taste.

You can also add ice cubes if you want a colder, thicker smoothie.

Blend all the ingredients until smooth and creamy.

Taste the smoothie and adjust the sweetness or spiciness by adding more honey, pineapple, or ginger if needed.

Pour the Coconut Pineapple Ginger Smoothie into two glasses and serve immediately.

Nutritional Information (per serving, without added sweeteners):

Calories: Approximately 150-200

Protein: About 2-3g

Fat: About 6-8g

Carbohydrates: About 25-30g

Fiber: About 3-4g

Sugars: About 15-20g

Ecco la ricetta per un "Smoothie al Tè Matcha con Latte di Mandorla":

Smoothie al Tè Matcha con Latte di Mandorla

Matcha Green Tea Smoothie with Almond Milk

Difficulty Level: ☐

Preparation Time: About 5 minutes

Servings: 2

Ingredients:

1 cup of unsweetened almond milk

1 teaspoon of matcha green tea powder

1 ripe banana

1 tablespoon of honey or maple syrup (optional, for sweetness)

1/2 teaspoon of vanilla extract (optional)

1 cup of ice cubes

Instructions:

Start by pouring one cup of unsweetened almond milk into a blender.

Add one teaspoon of matcha green tea powder to the milk.

Peel a ripe banana and add it to the blender.

If desired, you can add one tablespoon of honey or maple syrup for sweetness.

You can also add half a teaspoon of vanilla extract for an aromatic touch.

Add one cup of ice cubes to the blender to chill your smoothie.

Blend all the ingredients until you achieve a smooth and creamy consistency.

Taste your matcha smoothie, and if needed, adjust the sweetness or consistency by adding more milk or ice.

Pour the smoothie into two glasses and serve immediately.

Nutritional Information (per serving, without optional sweetener):

Calories: Approximately 100-150

Proteins: Approximately 2-3g

Fats: Approximately 3-5g

Carbohydrates: Approximately 20-25g

Fiber: Approximately 3-4g

Sugars: Approximately 10-15g

Kiwi and Fresh Mint Smoothie

- Difficulty Level: ☐
- Preparation Time: Approximately 5 minutes
- Servings: 2

Ingredients:

- 2 kiwis, peeled and chopped

- *1 cup of Greek yogurt*
- *1/2 cup of milk (you can use almond milk or coconut milk if preferred)*
- *1-2 tablespoons of honey (or sweetener of choice)*
- *Several fresh mint leaves*
- *Ice cubes (optional)*

Instructions:

1. *Start by peeling the kiwis and chopping them into pieces.*

2. *Place the kiwi pieces in a blender.*

3. *Add one cup of Greek yogurt.*

4. *Pour half a cup of milk into the blender. You can adjust the amount of milk according to your desired consistency.*

5. *Add one or two tablespoons of honey or sweetener of your choice. Adjust the amount of sweetener to your personal taste.*

6. *Add several fresh mint leaves to the blender. The amount of mint can vary depending on how intensely you want the mint flavor.*

7. *If desired, add some ice cubes to the blender to make the smoothie even more refreshing.*

8. *Blend all the ingredients until you achieve a smooth and homogeneous consistency.*

9. *Taste the smoothie, and if necessary, adjust the sweetener or consistency by adding more milk or ice.*

10. *Pour the kiwi and fresh mint smoothie into two glasses and garnish it with some extra mint leaves if desired.*

11. *Here are the approximate nutritional values for one serving of the Kiwi and Fresh Mint Smoothie (without optional ice):*

Calories: About 150-200

Protein: About 7-10g

Fat: About 2-3g

Carbohydrates: About 30-35g

Fiber: About 2-4g

Sugars: About 25-30g

Please note that these values are approximate and can vary based on the specific brands and types of ingredients used.

Enjoy your Kiwi and Fresh Mint Smoothie, rich in vitamin C and freshness!

CONCLUSION

Healthy Meal Prep: The Cookbook for a Healthy and Delicious Life" is a work created with the goal of helping you plan healthy, tasty, and convenient meals. The recipes contained herein have been carefully selected not only for their delicious taste but also for their adaptability to meal prep.

One of the distinctive features of these recipes is their ability to be prepared in advance, easily stored, and transported wherever you wish. Whether you're looking to save time in the kitchen during the week or planning meals to take to the office or the gym, you'll find that every dish here offers endless opportunities for customization.

All the recipes are designed to be flexible and versatile. You can prepare them well in advance, store them in the refrigerator or freezer, or even take them with you in convenient lunch containers. The key is to choose the right containers to meet your specific needs.

Here are some general guidelines for meal prep:

Choose the Right Containers: For storing dry meals like salads, opt for airtight containers. For dishes with sauces or soups, make sure the containers are leak-proof. If you plan to reheat meals in a microwave, ensure the containers are microwave-safe.

Label and Date: To keep track of the freshness of your meals, label each container with the name of the dish and the preparation date. This way, you'll always be aware of what you're about to consume.

Freeze for Long-Term Storage: If you've prepared a large quantity of meals, the freezer is your best friend. Freeze the

meals in single or family-sized portions, ensuring they'll be ready to thaw when you need them.

Be Creative: Many of these recipes are easily customizable. You can substitute ingredients or adjust portions to fit your preferences and nutritional needs.

Portability: Some meals are meant to be transported. Make sure to use sturdy containers that won't leak and that fit your on-the-go lifestyle.

In conclusion, "Healthy Meal Prep" offers you a range of recipes that allow you to be the director of your meals. Whether you want to plan meals for the entire week or simply prepare something quick and healthy to take with you, you'll find the inspiration you need in this cookbook.

Begin your journey to a healthier and tastier life through meal preparation. Control over what you eat has never been so delicious. Enjoy your meal!

Made in United States
North Haven, CT
22 January 2024

47781790R00091